THE MISSION DRIVEN HANDBOOK

A Resource for Moving from Profit to Purpose

Laura
Gassner
Otting

elevate

This publication is designed to provide accurate and authoritative information in regard to the subject matter covered. It is sold with the understanding that the publisher is not engaged in rendering legal, accounting, or other professional service. If legal advice or other expert assistance is required, the services of a competent professional should be sought.

Editorial Content: AnnaMarie McHargue
Cover Designer: Arthur Cherry

Published by Elevate Publishing, Boise, ID

Printed in the United States of America

April 2015
07 08 09 10 9 8 7 6 5 4 3 2 1

Library of Congress Cataloging-in-Publication Data

ISBN: 978-1937498672

DEDICATION

This book is dedicated to Eli J. Segal, who taught me that
increasing the bottom line means nothing if you aren't also
building a better world, and to Arnie Miller, without whom, I
would never have started this journey.

TABLE OF CONTENTS

Introduction vii

Chapter 1: Job Search 101 1

    Skills, Experience, Education, and Interests Assessment

    Networking: It's All about Whom You Know

    Job-Hunting Resources

Chapter 2: Building Your Nonprofit Résumé 35

    Corporate Résumés Differ from Nonprofit Résumés

    Making Your Résumé Work with Skills from Your Corporate Career

    Chronological versus Functional: Which Résumé Format Is for You?

    The Nonprofit Résumé: What to Include and What Not to Include

    Steps You Can Take to Improve Your New Nonprofit Résumé

Chapter 3: Cover Letters, Interviews, and References 75

    The Importance of Cover Letters

    Answering the Salary Question

    Mastering the Nonprofit Interview

    The Interview's Over: Now What?

    Strategic References

Epilogue 108

Appendix 111

INTRODUCTION

In my executive search practice I regularly am asked the following questions by individuals looking to transition from the corporate to the nonprofit sector:

- Is now the right time for me to transition into the nonprofit sector?
- What do I want to do, and where do I want to do it?
- Will my skills transfer to mission-driven work?
- What is working in the nonprofit sector really like?
- How do I deal with the financial ramifications of a nonprofit salary?
- Where do I even begin?

I wrote *Mission Driven*, and the companion text, *The Mission Driven Handbook,* to answer all of those questions and more.

The nonprofit sector is burgeoning with opportunities for career changers. Students are graduating from colleges and universities with bachelor's or master's degrees in nonprofit management. Midcareer professionals are looking around for a better work-life balance in careers that matter to them. Retiring baby boomers are finding that they are not so retiring after all. And the nonprofit sector is changing to accommodate the enormous richness of experience all of these individuals can bring with them. These books endeavor to help each of them find their place in the new nonprofit sector.

Mission Driven helps you assess whether the nonprofit sector is right for you and where in this vast sector you can find your place. The accompanying text, *The Mission Driven Handbook*, explores the finer details of how you should conduct your search, with specific tips and tools to enable you to network effectively, write a better résumé, craft more enticing cover letters, and interview as though you've been in the sector for ages. The handbook also includes a compendium of helpful resources, including job-posting websites, education programs, and knowledge tools.

Throughout these books, you will meet others who have made this transition before you. Many of them describe their transition as the best decision they ever made. You will, too.

Welcome to the nonprofit sector! We're glad you are here.

Laura Gassner Otting
Nonprofit Professionals Advisory Group
November 2006
Updated September 2014

CHAPTER 1:
Job Search 101

In *Mission Driven*, the first in this two-part series on transitioning to the nonprofit sector, corporate transitioners learned about the sector, both about trends affecting the sector as a whole and about specific nonprofits bringing tried and true models or innovative new solutions to intractable social problems. We discussed disadvantages and advantages to working in the nonprofit sector, and walked through a series of questions to determine if the nonprofit sector is the right move for you, at this time in your career and at this time in your life. We also dispelled many myths about the sector and drew up strategies to combat the stereotypes you might face as a corporate transitioner. We talked about dealing with the financial implications of earning a nonprofit salary. Finally, we discussed the explosive growth in jobs in the nonprofit sector, and how to find both your place in the nonprofit sector and a job in the nonprofit of your choice.

Having read *Mission Driven*, you should now have a greater understanding of the breadth, depth, and promise of the nonprofit sector. Let's now start looking for your perfect job: you want a new job, and you want it to be in the nonprofit sector, so, you're ready to start sending out your résumé, right? Not so fast.

Most job seekers make the mistake of thinking that they are ready to apply for a job (in any sector) simply because they need or want a new one. Yet nothing is more frustrating to a hiring manager than an unprepared candidate, and nothing will more quickly sink your chances of making the sector switch than a poorly executed job search. You've likely done a lot of thinking about, or are interested in exploring deeper, what a career in the nonprofit sector might mean for you. The first thing you need to do is to make sure that your candidacy reflects that.

In addition, you need to make sure that your collateral materials and your networking, interviewing, and references reflect your internalization of the transition as well. Throughout this book, we will endeavor to ensure that you have a résumé created—or built through additional service and education—that puts you in good standing to work in the sector at your highest and best level of contribution. But, we will also discuss cover letters, a key piece of artillery in your search, one that answers important questions and dispels any stereotypes surrounding your candidacy. We will discuss how to answer tricky questions around salary, and how to master the nonprofit interview, whether in networking, as an informational interview, or through follow up. Lastly, we'll talk about how to strategically deploy your references to be your best champions in this transition.

Let's get you started, now, in Job Search 101. Hiring managers expect that you, as the job seeker, are doing everything in your power to present your best self during your job search. Any misstep makes them worry, *If this is you at your best and I'm questioning your ability, your knowledge, your preparedness, what will you be like when you've been on the job for a year, or if you've got a personal crisis at home distracting you, or if I don't keep you motivated, or if you are asked to work a bit too hard during a crunch time?* You can and should avoid this reaction by being polished and prepared, knowing yourself and your experience, understanding deeply the nonprofit sector and the challenges you will face, and being the best candidate you can be. This chapter will help you do just that.

For better or for worse, as a candidate coming from the corporate world, you will have to jump over a higher hurdle than traditional nonprofit candidates to make your transition seem possible. There are stereotypes to correct, knowledge to gain, and a whole new language to master. Coming to the interview chair prepared to address these issues will make all the difference between a successful job search and one that lands you right back where you started.

Skills, Experience, Education, and Interests Assessment

Let's begin by determining what kind of job you want. Before you start your job search, make sure you distinguish between what you *want* to do and what you are *qualified* to do. The answers to these two questions are often completely different. But don't be afraid of that divergence.

The nonprofit sector is filled with people who come from nontraditional, nonlinear careers. Dropping out of a Wall Street lifestyle to move to Africa to help save endangered animals won't make you an anomaly in the nonprofit sector. Don't shy away from something that might seem far out. Instead, keep an open mind, think broadly, and adapt your job search accordingly.

Nine Questions to Guide Your Job Search

Knowing you want to work in the nonprofit sector is easy. It's often been described by career changers as something they couldn't not do. It's a fire in the pit of your stomach, a yearning for more, a decision that life is more than a paycheck. Yet figuring out just where you fit into this vast and wide-ranging sector is not so easy. The following questions will help you begin to determine where and what you can do.

1. What skills are in your toolbox?

Knowing what you can do and what you have done is important, but don't get trapped by your current title or your current job. After all, it's the job you're looking to leave, likely for good reason. Simply replicating your corporate job in the nonprofit sector gets you no more than a smaller paycheck. Think more deeply about what you do now and what you have done in other jobs so that your career change choices reflect the whole you, not just the most recent version.

On your résumé, remember to include work you may have done as a member of an ad hoc office committee, regardless of whether it involved your official line duties or not. Examine your projects and highlight any and all skills you have developed by completing each of the tasks involved. Regardless of how relevant these skills and tasks seem to your current job, they may matter greatly in your next one.

2. *Where did you collect the experiences you will bring to your next job?*

Not all experiences are gained through paid employment. Rather, much of the most fulfilling, most educational, and most relevant experience for the nonprofit job you seek may have come from volunteer work. Meaningful work is meaningful work, whether or not you got paid.

Looking at the larger collection of skills is particularly relevant for those just coming back into the workplace after getting an advanced degree or caring for a family member, or who have held the same job for a lengthy period of time. A certain amount of amnesia sets in, and a malaise about qualifications is not uncommon. Dusting off the old résumé and tacking on your most recent job does a disservice to you and your job hunt. Add all of your experiences, paid or volunteer, to the equation when determining the full scope of skills you bring to bear. They may add up to more than you think.

3. *What would you do, if you could do anything at all?*

As you have learned in the accompaniment to this book, *Mission Driven*, the nonprofit sector is enormous and varied. You can do virtually anything you want to do in a nonprofit that exists and, if not, start one of your own. Consider this the famous question: "If you won the lottery, what would you do tomorrow?"

Allow yourself to dream, and dream big. After all, if you are moving into the nonprofit sector to fulfill that certain something inside of you, why not go all the way? The time is now, and the price is right. Besides, the nonprofit sector is filled with dreamers just like you. You can always scale back or get creative when faced with unexpected realities that crop up during your job search. But until that happens, allow yourself to be carried away by the fantasy of making real change in the issue area or community of your choice. You will find that your enthusiasm is infectious and will excite those around you to help you more.

4. *Which of your skills will transfer into the nonprofit sector?*

Some skills transfer more easily than others. Most duties that fall under the operations, administration, and finance functions are easily transferable, even if there are some new rules or technology to learn. Some, like community building and fund development, can transfer well after a bit of tweaking. Other skills, those heavily reliant on subject matter expertise, are much more difficult to fit into your new nonprofit job, unless the nonprofit focuses in that area. For example, a marketing director focused on selling to educational outfits may be able to bring a quiver filled with both functional and subject matter arrows to a job raising money for a charter school association. On the other hand, an eye doctor will bring a deep understanding of the medical community and its support of blind children, but a lifetime of clinical expertise will not apply when budgeting, dealing with funders, or signing off on press releases. Those skills must (and can) come from elsewhere.

Many of skills you have gathered are likely transferable to the nonprofit sector. However, before starting to write your résumé, make sure that the skills you think will transfer are in line with the requirements of the new position or the level of position you seek. The eye doctor just discussed, for example, might point to a track record running a successful, 200-patient practice, developing community support around an eye care program in local schools, and lobbying the state to earmark funds to an "Eye Care for the Elderly" program.

5. What traits have brought you success?

In most cases, subject matter expertise is only part of what has enabled you to succeed in your career thus far. Your personality, the way you go about doing your work or managing the work of others, and your general demeanor in the office complete the picture. You may be the type of person who operates well under pressure and in turnaround situations, or you may be better in a more stable environment where crises rarely pop up. You may be able to get the best from legions of young, idealistic, energetic upstarts, or you may be more skilled at managing a smaller cadre of seasoned professionals. You may enjoy a highly charged political atmosphere, or you may thrive, instead, in an environment where agendas are more transparent.

Each nonprofit has its own personality. Some of these personalities reflect the organization's issue area. For example, human rights organizations tend to be more activist, with younger, idealistic staffers, while institutions of higher education tend to be more reserved. Yet in each of these categories, there are always exceptions. Discerning what environment brings out your best traits and allows you to flourish, and finding a nonprofit that offers such an environment, will allow you better to enjoy your nonprofit work.

6. What type of formal education do you have?

Without a great deal of work experience, formal education determines what, substantively speaking, you are qualified to do. This is the whole of your subject matter expertise. For those just coming out of school, or with only one job under their belts, education is of paramount importance and will be weighted heavily by the hiring manager. What you know matters, and what you know has mainly come from schooling at this point.

**Determine Your Functional Areas Expertise:
Where Do Your Capabilities Lie?**

Your functional areas of expertise are those things that you can do well, either because of experience or study. These determine the type of role you might fill in a nonprofit organization.

- ☐ Accounting and finance
- ☐ Activism and organizing
- ☐ Administration
- ☐ Advertising
- ☐ Architecture
- ☐ Clerical and data entry
- ☐ Computers and technology
- ☐ Construction
- ☐ Counseling
- ☐ Customer service
- ☐ Database management
- ☐ Direct social services
- ☐ Driving
- ☐ Editing and writing
- ☐ Education and training
- ☐ Employment and human services
- ☐ Engineering
- ☐ Event planning

- ☐ Food service
- ☐ Fundraising and development
- ☐ Gardening
- ☐ Grants administration
- ☐ Graphic design
- ☐ Health and medical
- ☐ Legal
- ☐ Library sciences
- ☐ Maintenance and janitorial
- ☐ Management
- ☐ Marketing
- ☐ Photography
- ☐ Project management
- ☐ Public relations
- ☐ Research
- ☐ Sales
- ☐ Telemarketing

For those who have been in the working world a bit longer, education is only one part of the equation. In some cases, like medicine or the law, a formal degree is a state requirement. Also, social workers and teachers must be licensed, and stock traders and accountants must pass certain exams. In other cases, like fundraising or association management, a degree or certificate is not a requirement but provides a leg up against other candidates. Determine what your formal education qualifies you to do and what degrees or certificates you might need to grab the job of your dreams.

Some managers, especially those in the foundation world, find that a deep, substantive knowledge of the work funded or being done by their grantees is vital to a candidate's success once on board. This is often borne out by a long career in the field or, for foundations, more likely a Ph.D. in the subject area. In some cases, however, attaining more education is unrealistic. You are unlikely to enter medical school when you are 45, although certainly it has been done, and

Questions to Determine Your Best Work Environment

The nonprofit sector is broad enough to include organizations with all different personalities. Determine what kind of work environment you need and where your skills and traits might blossom by considering the following questions. Remember: there are no right or wrong answers.

Yes No

☐ ☐ **Do you like to know what you will face each morning when you walk into the office?**

☐ ☐ **Do you enjoy the thrill of a new and possibly unknown challenge each day?**

☐ ☐ **Do you prefer to work in a hands-on capacity, creating and seeing change up close and personal in the lives of one individual at a time?**

☐ ☐ **Would you rather make change from a distance, at a more strategic level, guiding larger programs that effect change in broader populations that you might not necessarily see every day?**

☐ ☐ **Do you function better in environments where the goals are straightforward and the results are measurable?**

☐ ☐ **Are you comfortable in a more amorphous role, where the goalposts are constantly changing and the field is ever in flux?**

☐ ☐ **Would you rather fill a position that has been held in the past by another, where the expectations are clear?**

☐ ☐ **Do you enjoy creating your own path, blazing a new trail, and introducing functions into an organization?**

☐ ☐ **Would you be able to perform a serious job in an organization where the majority of staff wear T-shirts and flip-flops to the office?**

☐ ☐ **Do you wear a tie even on casual Friday, preferring a serious, staid atmosphere?**

☐ ☐ **Are you an individual decision maker who can quickly determine the correct solution without much input from others?**

☐ ☐ **Do you prefer to get the opinions of all around you, weighing pros and cons and talking until consensus is reached?**

Many different types of personality and traits tests are available that can help you determine what your "organizational personality" might be. From Myers-Briggs to the Enneagram to Jung's theory on personality types, the Internet is a vast and wonderful world of self-help right at your fingertips. Try a few of these personality tests on for size. You might be surprised at what you find, but you'll also be better prepared to find the nonprofit that is right for you.

you are probably not going to get a Ph.D. in oceanography to work at the Jacques Cousteau Foundation (however fun that may seem).

In other cases, degrees that teach skills and not subject matter expertise, such as programs on nonprofit management, fundraising, accounting, and operations, are easily attainable and make sense strategically. This type of education provides you with a current nonprofit peer group, access to a career center, and a mind filled with the best nonprofit thinking of the day. The second half of this chapter discusses additional educational resources in more detail.

7. What kinds of on-the-job training have you received?

Many job seekers have received enough on-the-job training to write a Ph.D. thesis on the work that they do. In most cases, however, they just don't realize how much they've learned along the way. Figuring this out demands critical thinking about where you came from, your initial expectations of your career's trajectory, and where you have ended up.

What did you hope to get from your career? Are you there? What changed along the way? What do you do now that you never imagined you would be doing? What more do you know now than when you started this job, or the last job, or the job before that? And, again, don't forget about the community service, nonprofit volunteering, or board work that you have done. Each of your days has brought a lesson, and each lesson is valuable to your job search in some way. What have been your lessons?

8. What motivates you to make this move?

If you are switching sectors, you may find yourself applying for jobs that seem completely unconnected to where you have been and what you are currently doing. However, a unique, often life-altering experience as a volunteer, an illness in the family, or a major world catastrophe are often exactly the right, and perfectly plausible, times to make such a dramatic change. If properly framed, your underlying motivation will make sense to the person judging your candidacy.

Consider those people looking for the nonprofit sector lifestyle: that idyllic world where people don't work that hard and go home early on Fridays, where accountability is scant and responsibility is shared, where everyone is kind and sweet and no one ever fights. That world is about as realistic as the mirage of an oasis in the desert. Times have changed, the nonprofit sector has changed, and the jobs within it have changed, too. Expect to work harder than you ever have but for a cause you deeply love.

Think about your underlying motivation to make this move. Is your motivation just a passing fancy that will flame out when met with rough times, frustration, and defeats? Or is it from deep within your core, empowering you to face down the difficulties inherent to the nonprofit sector, so that you may make an organization's dream a reality for all? Ask yourself tough questions about how you really feel about this major career change and keep asking until you feel you have

Figure Out Your Issue Area:

What Interests You, What Excites You, What Must You Impact?

Determine the difference between what interests you and what drives you. Knowing that your job search may not be linear and that you may have to expand your options to move to your perfect job in stages, divide this list into the following categories:

- **No, work in this issue area doesn't excite me (N).**

- **I might find work in this issue area interesting (M).**

- **I yearn to be part of the change in this issue area (Y).**

___Advocacy

___AIDS/HIV

___Arts and culture

___Associations

___Children and youth

___Community-building and renewal

___Community service

___Computers and the Internet

___Consumer protection

___Corporate social responsibility

___Crime and safety

___Disability

___Disaster relief

___Diversity

___Economic development

___Education (preschool)

___Education (K-12)

___Education (college and university)

___Energy conservation

___Environment

___Family and parenting

___Farming and agriculture

___Foundations and philanthropy

___Gay, lesbian, bisexual, and transgender

___Government and politics

___Government oversight and reform

___Health policy

___Health services

___Housing and homelessness

___Human rights and civil liberties

___Human services

___Immigration

___International issues

___Job training and workplace issues

___Labor movement

___Legal assistance

___Library and resource centers

___Media and publishing

___Men and boys

___Mental health

___Multiservice community agency

___Network of nonprofit organizations

___Nutrition/hunger

___Peace and conflict resolution

___Personal finance

___Philanthropy

___Poverty

___Prison reform

___Public authority

___Public policy

___Public relations/communications

___Public-private partnerships

___Race and ethnicity

___Recovery, addiction, and abuse

___Recreation, sports, and leisure

___Religion and faith-based organizations

___Rural issues

___Security/defense

___Seniors and retirement

___Social justice

___Social services

___Spiritual and metaphysical issues

___Technology

___Transportation

___Veterans

___Voting and enfranchisement

___Wildlife and animal welfare

___Women's issues

an honest answer. This is what will drive your job search, your enthusiasm, and your ability to make change a reality.

9. Why is this the right time for you to move into this new type of work?

Your children may have left the nest, you may have a sick relative, you may be unable to stomach one more day of corporate profiteering, or you may have benefited greatly from your career and can now write your own rules. Everyone has their reasons, and all of them are real and valid. However, only some of them should influence your job search. The timing must have everything to do with how a particular job, including the lifestyle and financial considerations that come with it, will play into your life at this time.

Perhaps your company is downsizing, and this is a move you have always desired. Perhaps you are a board member for a nonprofit whose chief executive just announced plans for retirement. Perhaps you are just coming back to work after raising your children, and because of that life-transforming experience, realize that you cannot go back to the job you held before. Realizing why this is the right time for you, for your family, and for your bank account is key to deciding which kind of job to seek.

Determine Which Job Is Right for You

As you may have noticed, these questions fall into different categories: professional experience, education, individual skills, and personal interests. None of these categories is mutually exclusive of another. For example, don't be fooled into thinking that just because you were educated as a lawyer means you have to practice law in the nonprofit sector. The education gained to become a lawyer is substantive and puts you in good standing to practice in your particular field of the law. However, the professional experience you may have gained as a lawyer and the individual attributes that have made you successful allow you to do so much more.

Lawyers learn to negotiate, mediate, research, and apply critical thinking in one area to another, to give but a few examples. Some have managed law practices with significant budgets and staff and have had to rid themselves of any shyness about asking for money. Most have had to market themselves and their abilities and have learned a great deal about public presentation, inside a courtroom and in the world at large. A good lawyer will have developed personal attributes such as the ability to talk to lay audiences and peers, patience with bureaucratic systems, and the perseverance to continue an argument when it looks as though all hope is lost. Combine that with the desire to change a community, state, or country, and you have yourself a pretty powerful nonprofit leader. Breaking down your career and the jobs you have held will yield a fruitful dossier for your nonprofit job search.

Don't Expect a Linear Path

Your move from the corporate sector to the nonprofit sector may take a few twists and turns before you find your dream job. In fact, you may have to make your move in stages, first for function, then for issue area, until you have amassed the right experience in your targeted area. For example, it is unlikely that you will go from a role as a senior financial analyst for General Electric to become the vice president for operations and finance for the Minnesota Human Services Coalition without a couple of jobs in between. You'd need to get experience regarding nonprofit operations, get a basic level of understanding about human services, learn more about nonprofit financial accounting, get a sense of Minnesota politics, and have a more senior perspective about nonprofits. The nine questions you just answered are designed to make you more strategic in choosing your next job, thereby minimizing the steps needed to get from here to there.

Networking: It's All about Whom You Know

In the corporate sector, the vast majority of jobs are filled through word of mouth. In the nonprofit sector, it is even more extreme. Advertising for an unexpected vacancy requires an unexpected allocation of money, and money, especially when it's needed unexpectedly, is in limited supply in the nonprofit sector. If a nonprofit can fill a job through the people in their network before spending a dollar on advertising, it will do so every time.

The Importance of Networking

Networking is important. Underline that sentence three times. There is simply no substitute in a job search, whether in the corporate or nonprofit sector. In fact, it is so vital to a successful job search that it bears repeating: *networking is important*.

A good rule of thumb is to spend 75 percent of your time networking—very little of which should be spent pursuing executive search firms directly—and only about 25 percent of your time answering advertisements found online or in the paper. You will find out about more opportunities that are currently available and soon to be available that way, and your candidacy will be taken more seriously. Consider this: if someone submitted a résumé to you because a mutual connection put you in touch, wouldn't you take that applicant more seriously than the one who responded, along with a hundred others, to the advertisement in the local newspaper? Of course you would—doing so is simple human nature, and you can easily use it to your advantage.

Before you get nervous that you are a corporate person with no ties to the nonprofit sector, think again. Everyone you know has some connection to a nonprofit. They may be involved with or members of the following:

- An alumni association
- A parent-teacher organization
- A neighborhood coalition
- A church, synagogue, or mosque
- A political campaign
- The Boy Scouts or Girl Scouts
- A citywide cleanup effort
- A local chorale or chamber music ensemble
- The Junior League
- Countless others

Each of these people knows scores of others who are involved with them, and each of them, in turn, knows scores more, and so on and so on. Suddenly, you have access to hundreds of potential connectors. By tapping into your existing network, you may find yourself surprisingly close to key decision makers in nonprofits of interest to you. Telling everyone you encounter about your search, then, will greatly increase the likelihood that you will be successful.

Similarly, each day you encounter many valuable resources that should be tapped for your job search. In addition to the individuals you know or meet, these resources may include networking associations, community organizations, or alumni groups, all of which may provide precious links to otherwise unknown opportunities. Figure out where you want to be and work backwards, creating a relational map to someone in that organization. Draw lines between connectors until you have found the person who makes the hiring decision. Then start taking advantage of these relationships and resources. You will be amazed at whom you know and whom they know.

Tips for Successful Networking

Networking can seem like an unpleasant assignment. You may feel as though you are bothering people or taking up their time with matters they do not care about or even understand. Truth be told, they have been there, too. Each of them once looked for a job, and each of them used some form of networking, large or small, in their job search. Furthermore, remember that you share a common interest: working in the nonprofit sector or issue area in general and perhaps that nonprofit organization in specific. Your enthusiasm for their work will carry the conversation.

Whether you relish the idea of networking or not, having some tools in your pocket will make it more fun.

Become Active in Your Issue Area of Choice

Hundreds of networking associations exist in every city, on almost every imaginable topic, from women executives, to grant writers, to outdoors enthusiasts, to left-handed unicyclists. Getting involved in one or more of these affinity groups is a surefire way to multiply your network in a targeted, quick, and efficient manner. Most of these groups have regular gatherings, job postings, and other valuable networking opportunities. Join every club you can and begin to accept any and all invitations that come your way.

In addition to providing a directly relevant group of contacts, involvement in your issue area of choice will teach you the appropriate lingo, keep you up to date on current trends and challenges, provide invitations to speaker forums or other events where leaders will be presenting, and introduce you to the movers and shakers in the field. The knowledge you gain will make you both more successful in your job search and more likely to hit the ground running once you are hired. Finally, this activity will begin to form a history on your résumé of real involvement, showing that you are serious about making a move.

Find a Buddy

Even in the best of circumstances, job searches are long, arduous, and often lonely processes. In fact, searching for the perfect job can take six months to a year, depending on what you are looking to do next and how well your past has prepared you. The added difficulty of moving from the corporate to the nonprofit sector will certainly add time as well.

It is easy to get discouraged and give up, especially if you are doing it alone. Setting up a regular session with a friend, coach, or job search counselor can renew your energy, rebuild your self-esteem, and keep you focused on the end game. Many professional networking associations have job seeker subgroups, which can prove to be both professionally and personally rewarding; undoubtedly, you will also find some job seekers in the personal affinity groups as well. Don't be shy about asking them to get together; they will be thrilled for the company.

Set Benchmarks of Success

Another great way to keep focused on your search is to give yourself homework. Try to set some benchmarks: make 20 calls per week, have coffee or lunch with someone every day, never let anyone off the phone without their giving you at least three more names, follow up within one week. Successful job searches thrive on momentum, and benchmarks like these will assure that you have it.

The first step is to create a list of names. Try to get as many as you can on paper, but don't let yourself off the hook until you've jotted down at least a few dozen. Write down the names of anyone with whom you currently work; worked in previous jobs; sit on a community committee; see in the car pool pickup line; or encounter where you worship, play sports, or ballroom dance. These are your first points of contact and the place to begin your networking. You can always remove names later (if, for example, you are unable to tell people at your current job just yet), but having these names written down now means you will be able to be more strategic about to whom and when you begin to go public with your job search.

Now let's talk about that strategy. My mentor, Arnie Miller, is one of the founders of the field of professional search for the nonprofit sector. For many years, I listened to him give career counsel and job seeking advice to those looking to make a change, whether within the nonprofit sector itself or into it for the first time. His advice is perfect. Look at your list of names, and divide it into three sections: those who can be most helpful to you, those who can be somewhat helpful to you, and those who can be least helpful. Then, start with those who can be the least helpful to you, for those are the ones with whom you want to practice your pitch and sharpen your strategy, and, yes, make your mistakes.

Walk in the Footsteps of Others

In your networking, keep an alert eye out for others who have already made the move from the corporate to the nonprofit sector. Finding a former corporate denizen happily ensconced in a nonprofit benefits you in many ways. First, you are more likely to get in the door, because the person behind it knows what you are going through. They may have been helped by someone along their way and want to pass along the good karma, or perhaps they were not helped at all and want to make life easier for those who are coming up behind them. Second, they will already understand where you are coming from, so you might not have to sell them quite as hard on why the nonprofit sector is the right place for someone with a business background.

As a successful career changer, they can then, in turn, be a credible advocate on your behalf. Third, you will be able to ask questions about breaking into the nonprofit sector, their particular nonprofit, and challenges that they faced in their own sector switch. The answers you get will contain acceptable language to use in your own answers when you ultimately get asked these same questions in interviews.

Don't Discount Your Corporate Contacts

According to the Bureau of Labor Statistics, in a report compiled by the Urban Institute, 62.6 million adults volunteered in the United States during 2013, which accounts for over 25[1] percent of the U.S. population. This means that the person in the next cubicle, despite having a career in the corporate sector, may spend time on the weekends volunteering at a local soup kitchen or serving on the board of the local zoo. Volunteering is hip, and it helps even corporate ladder climbers get ahead. You, too, can use this to your advantage by hitting up your corporate contacts for their nonprofit connections.

Keep Detailed Notes

If you are truly networking as much as you should be, you will get confused about where people are working, what they are doing, to whom they have referred you, and the purpose of their organization. Remember that most people work at a particular nonprofit to serve its mission. It is more than a bit insulting—and will come across as patronizing from someone in the corporate sector—to mix up one nonprofit's mission with another's.

Buy a notebook into which you staple business cards. Set up a database on your computer. Create index cards. Draw giant maps on your walls connecting contacts to each other and, ultimately, to your dream job. Do whatever you need to do to keep your networking straight. Your airtight organizational skills will be seen as a laser-like passion for the mission and a deep respect for those who work to fulfill it.

Be Clear and Concise

Arm your networking contacts with the ability to help you by giving them clear and concise directions on what, specifically, they can do for you. One of the biggest mistakes a job seeker can make is to ask for general help and hope, expect, or assume that their contacts will do the math for them. That doesn't happen.

If you aren't concise and clear with your needs, you will still get promises of help but, in reality, will be leaving your contacts with little or no tools to follow through. Your contacts have limited enough time that burdening them with extra work—for example, figuring out what your skills and experiences add up to—will generate frustration and failure. No matter how much they want to help, they will be unable to do so.

Be clear. Be concise. Above all, give your contacts specific requests to which they can respond.

---

1. Urban Institute Center on Nonprofits and Philanthropy, "The Nonprofit Sector in Brief 2013," Page 1.

Opportunities: Lost and Gained

- **Lost opportunity.** "I'd like to move into the nonprofit sector and think I could do good for lots of different kinds of organizations. Do you know anyone who is hiring?"

- **Gained opportunity.** "After ten years of honing my skills in brand management in corporate America, I've decided that I'd like to dedicate myself to what has always been a passion of mine: leadership training for girls, preferably in the junior high school years. I know that you have been active in the Girl Scouts, and I think my experience would transfer well into their organization-wide efforts to create more chapters. Whom do you think I should call to begin networking into the right circles? Where is the most innovative thinking in the sector right now? Do you know of any organizations that have these types of jobs, whether filled or vacant, where I can connect to like-minded individuals?"

Be careful not to treat a networking opportunity like an informational interview. Informational interviews, discussed later in this chapter, are wonderful opportunities to delve more deeply into how your contact sees your skills and expertise, how they think you might be able to transition into the sector, and what they feel is missing from your résumé at present. Informational interviews should include the usual networking questions, of course, but networking should never include informational interview questions. If you trap someone expecting a quick networking encounter in a long conversation—especially at an event where they have their own networking expectations and agenda—yours won't be a welcome phone call later on. Keep it light, keep it quick, and always ask if you can call them to follow up with an informational interview later.

The Sector Switcher's Elevator Speech

Imagine that you've just stepped into an elevator only to find, unguarded by her brick wall of an assistant, the woman with whom you've been trying unsuccessfully for months to land an interview, a telephone conversation, or even just a returned phone call. You have no more than maybe 11 floors, or 15 to 30 seconds, to make your case. What are you going to say to her? Hence, the so-called "elevator speech." Thankfully, most networking elevator speeches are delivered under far less pressure, but being prepared, no matter what life throws at you, will enable you to deliver this information in a casual but impressive manner.

The typical elevator speech includes a little about you and a little about what you want to do next. Yours must have more. The sector switcher's elevator speech includes answers to four key questions:

1. Who are you?

2. What do you do currently?

3. What makes you an interesting and likely successful sector switcher (e.g., your volunteer work, additional education, board responsibilities, or passions)?

4. What do you want to do now and why?

Remember to include more than just the "what" in your speech but the "why" as well. It is the burning question on the mind of anyone interested in hiring you and can and should be answered in both of its forms: "Why this mission?" and "Why now?" Gauge your level of sentimentality for your particular audience; some may be amazed that you harbor this secret love for their mission, but some may find your emotions too personal and too revealing all at once.

Example #1: With a Potential Employer

"Hi, my name is Ellen Torres. I'm currently the chief of investor relations for State Street Capital, Ltd. While my day job has honed my ability to craft excellent communications for corporate investors, my volunteering has shown me that my real passion lies in caring for our aging population. I'm currently looking for a position where I can combine my expert public relations knowledge with my passion for our nation's greatest living treasure, the elderly. I saw your announcement for a director of communications and would love to set up a time where we can meet to discuss what I can do for you. What is the best way to contact you?"

Example #2: At a Career Fair

"Hello, my name is Max Vonhaven. I've been working for the past five years as a computer engineer for a regional supermarket chain. I helped design and implement a data management system for multisite operations across four different states. On the side, I've gotten involved in our corporate volunteering effort with Habitat for Humanity. I see that you are looking for someone to build your technology capacity as you expand your house-building efforts regionally, and know that I can bring the right skills to help you do that. Here is my résumé. Can we set up a time where I can tell you more about how I can help you get to where you'd like to be?"

Example #3: Over Dinner with Friends, Family, or Acquaintances

"I've decided that I am going to make the leap to the nonprofit sector, and I'd like to enlist your help. As you know, this is a natural progression of my career, because I have been performing many of the tasks associated with the jobs that I want for the past 25 years. I am focusing my job search at the executive director level in organizations that focus on one of my three areas of passion: getting young people involved in politics, leadership programs for women and girls, and community service. Whom do you think I should call to further explore this dream of mine?"

Practice, practice, practice your speech. In fact, remove the "speech" from the speech. Make it a conversation opener, not a monologue. It should roll off your tongue and be natural, not memorized or stilted. Say it to your friends, your neighbors, your parakeet. This is the first time people are imagining you in this different role, and your ability to seem natural in its presentation will affect their interest in helping you get there.

Be Thankful

Unfortunately, some corporate job seekers see their decision to work for less money as a favor they are bestowing upon the nonprofit sector. The nonprofit sector doesn't see it that way. A few bad apples have left a bad taste in the mouths of many nonprofit hiring managers. Be sure to be thankful along the way to avoid being tagged as an ungrateful job seeker.

Collect business cards from or make notes of the people with whom you interact during a job search. Send thank-you notes to each and every one of them, even if they were not all that helpful. They probably think they were, and telling them so will make them willing to try harder next time. Saying thank you will allow you to call them up repeatedly for advice, counsel, and new ideas without fear of reproach or dismissal.

Use your thank-you notes as strategic opportunities to share more information, make your case again, or simply say something you may have forgotten in a rushed encounter. A thank-you note is a perfect and (sadly) unexpected opportunity to thank an interviewer (even for an informational interview) for spending time with you and to remind them of your strengths. Tell them about your search and, specifically, what you would like them to do for you. If appropriate, enclose an additional or updated copy of your résumé.

Never forget about thanking your networking contacts or those who have agreed to be references for you in your job search. Thank-you notes to them are not only surprising but keep you and your job search fresh in their minds for longer. Remember, even if your contacts want deep in their hearts to assist you, you are not their first priority, and they will tend to forget. Don't be shy about reminding them gently how they can fulfill their wishes to help. Even if they were unable to come through for you on this job search, there will be others, and thanking them profusely, even for doing nothing, puts you in good standing for next time.

Informational Interviews

Throughout your networking, you should be asking both for additional connections and informational interviews. Informational interviews enable you to accomplish several things at once. They allow you to:

- Introduce yourself to someone who may have a job opening in the future
- Learn more about the people who work at this nonprofit
- Receive direction and guidance from someone who was once in your shoes
- Learn a name to drop in your networking and personal connections you can use
- Gain valuable insights from an insider about trends in the sector in general, this nonprofit specifically, and the language to use to describe both
- Hear about some concerns, assumptions, or stereotypes that might be affecting your sector switch and how you might combat them
- Audition some preliminary answers to obvious interview questions when a particular job isn't on the line

Informational interviews can be a great boon to your job search if done well. If done poorly, however, they can only hinder your transition. Beware of the following "major don'ts" as you embark on your informational interviews.

Major Don't #1: Asking for a Job

One thing you are not seeking from an informational interview, ironically enough, is a job. You are there to get information. You will talk about your skills and experience and why you think you could be right for the nonprofit sector, and, of course, you will leave your résumé. But this isn't a job interview. You are the interviewer, not the interviewee. Bring some directed questions, but mostly listen to what your interviewee has to say. If you seem right for the organization, and there is an opening, rest assured that your interviewee will put two and two together and move your résumé along to the right person.

That being said, come prepared for an informational interview as if it were an interview where you might land a real job. You never know if it might turn into one. Most jobs are not advertised, and many employers do not even realize they have a need until they meet a person who might fill it. Be ready with great answers, extra copies of your résumé, and an open mind so that you can pivot quickly to the interview chair if the opportunity arises.

Major Don't #2: Disrespecting Their Time

Never ask to meet for coffee or lunch—even if it's your treat—unless the time is offered to you. It is a bigger time commitment than the person might want or be able to make, and likely they value that time more than the $6.95 sandwich they would get out of the deal. Instead, offer to come to their office for a 15-minute conversation. Everyone has 15 minutes, and the easier you make the interview for them, the more likely they are to give it to you.

To keep your contacts motivated to help you, never give the impression that your time is more important than their time. Be ever conscious of how much time you are taking. Disrespecting the 15 minutes you were granted by asking question upon question will turn a friend into a foe or, at the very least, a complacent contact. Complacent contacts don't open up and hand over names of their friends and colleagues, lest you commit the same time-sucking crime with them, too.

Major Don't #3: Being Unprepared

A huge mistake many informational interviewers (that's you) make is to assume that this is a chance to get basic information about an organization. Don't waste your time or the interviewee's time by asking them to tell you basic things that you could have found out by conducting the most limited research. They won't feel as though you value the opportunity to speak with them and will feel undervalued, even insulted, as a result.

Arriving at an informational interview with more than basic knowledge about the person or the organization is more then just impressive; it's essential. It makes you ask smarter questions. Be creative, be ingenious, and put information you've learned about them and their organization together with other information you've gathered elsewhere. You will look more intelligent and more like someone they might take a chance on introducing around, either at their own office or to friends who might have job openings.

Major Don't #4: Talking Too Much

You come to an interview to learn from the person on the other side of the desk, not vice versa. Avoid the temptation to jump into the conversation as soon as you see an opportunity to talk about your skills and how great a job you would do in the nonprofit sector. Remember, studies show that people who talk more in conversations think that those conversations went very well. Why not give your interviewee a chance to be a "great conversationalist," leaving a positive impression about you while at the same time getting valuable data about the organization and the nonprofit sector?

Bring specific questions and allow your interviewee to answer them. Be prepared to be asked questions, too. You'll want to be able to pinpoint what you'd like to do and where you'd like to do it, but make sure you are using most of the time to learn more from them than they from you. There will always be another time for them to interview you if they are impressed from your first conversation.

Major Don't #5: Not Listening

You are getting this time as a gift; use it wisely. Don't ask the obvious, and avoid asking the same question over again. If you've run out of questions, say thank you and leave. It's that simple. You can always call back later if you think of more questions. However, if you seem as though you are fishing around to fill time because you are unprepared or because you were unfocused for the first few minutes, your follow-up calls will likely go unreturned.

Pay exceptional amounts of attention to what the interviewee is telling you, but treating this opportunity like a college lecture with a quiz coming tomorrow will come across as strange and stilted. Take notes as needed but not so much that you fail to converse normally.

Ten Smart Questions to Ask at an Informational Interview

You are unlikely to get all of your questions answered in an informational interview, so be direct about your most important ones. The smarter the questions, the smarter the questioner looks.

1. What brought you to this nonprofit and this mission area? In what ways has it lived up to your expectations? In what ways have you been disappointed?

2. I read with great interest about how your organization is expanding programs into four new states. This is particularly interesting to me as an entrepreneur. Can you tell me about the funding challenges that poses and how, given current philanthropic trends, you are planning to handle them?

3. Whom do you consider to be your competition for funding, for media, for members?

4. What is the working atmosphere like here? Is this typical for the nonprofit sector in your experience? What do you enjoy, and what do you dislike?

5. I notice that many of the staff here, like you, have business backgrounds. What difficulties did that pose to you when you came into the nonprofit sector? In what ways did it make things easier? (Or, conversely, I notice that few of the staff have business backgrounds and wonder how you feel about the ability of people to switch sectors?)

6. Which skills, experiences, backgrounds, or personality types have you found to be most successful in your role? Which have not?

7. How has this organization and your role changed since you've been here? In response to what? How does it need to continue to change?

8. How would you assess my background, and where would you think I ought to focus my professional development to be successful in the type of position I seek?

9. Do you have any words of wisdom, advice, or warning based on your experiences? What do you wish you knew when you started that you know now? Who else might have valuable insights and a good network of friends and colleagues?

10. May I follow up with you as my job search evolves to keep you posted and get additional advice along the way?

Job-Hunting Resources

Many new resources are available for job hunters, thanks to technology and to the enormous growth of the nonprofit sector. There are resources to help you get connected, get headhunted, get active, and get smart. In fact, from face-to-face conversations to Internet research to virtual networks, a good job seeker has more tools than time to use them.

Before you start using these resources, however, make sure that you have some tools of your own already set up. Strip your answering machine of any music, children's voices, or silly outgoing messages. Invest in faster computer access or learn the hours of local libraries, Wi-fi-enabled coffee shops, or public access technology centers. Find a fax number, like one at a local copy shop, so that you can give it out if asked. Set up an e-mail account with a serious outgoing address that you use for this and only this purpose. Treat your job search as if it is your job, and you will find yourself being taken more seriously.

Getting Connected: The Internet Is Your Playground

There is no better resource for today's job seeker than the Internet. With the thousands of job announcements, networking groups, membership lists, and websites spoon-feeding you all the data you need for a successful job search, it is nearly impossible to go wrong. Yet the Internet can be overwhelming if you fail to use it in a constructive and strategic manner.

Online Job Boards

The Internet has been overrun with recruiters and human resource managers trawling for the best candidate catch. Their bait is placed on webpages large and small, nonprofit and corporate, exclusive to the nonprofit world and not. But you can't bite until you find their hooks, and that's not always easy.

Literally hundreds of sites on the Internet list jobs. There are the big ones, like Monster.com, CareerBuilder.com, and Indeed.com, and there are small ones that list jobs in specific fields or only in certain geographic areas. You should spend limited time trolling around the big sites and pay more attention to the smaller, more directed ones. This may seem counterintuitive, but let's consider the facts.

CareerXRoads, a highly respected publication that ranks job boards by popularity, produced an alarming study in 2001 that showed hiring rates in the single digits from big online boards, but recommissioned the study in 2013 to find an upward trend. The numbers are still quite low at just over 18 percent. On the other hand, entrepreneurs seeking profit and/or social change have invaded the nonprofit job search universe with dynamic, directed, cost-effective job boards. Ranging from sites that list the full range of available jobs across the nonprofit spectrum to sites that list jobs only in certain mission areas or functional expertise—like social work, education, or accounting and finance—there are job boards in this sector that make sense for your search.

Nonprofit Job Boards

Here are a few major nonprofit job boards that will act as great launching points for your job search journey.

- **www.idealist.org.** A project of Action Without Borders, Idealist is the granddaddy of nonprofit job boards. At $60 a posting for employers, it's considered a "can't miss" by most nonprofits. There are job postings from upwards of 45,000 nonprofit organizations in 180 countries in addition to volunteer and internship opportunities, events, resources, and programs.

- **http://philanthropy.com.** The Chronicle of Philanthropy is the newspaper of the nonprofit world. It is the number-one news source, in print and online, for charity leaders, fundraisers, grant makers, and others involved in the philanthropic enterprise. Each week, the Chronicle sends more than 168,000 e-mail messages to more than 15,000 users of this service.

- **www.execsearches.com.** Since its launch in 1999, ExecSearches.com has been a leader in mid- to senior-level job announcements with up to 400,000 visits per month from professionals seeking employment in nonprofits, the public sector, education, health, and the government.

- **www.nptimes.com**. The NonProfit Times covers the business of the nonprofit sector. Published in print 24 times a year, it is read by over 78,000 full-time nonprofit executive managers around the country.

- **www.associationjobs.com.** CEO Update posts jobs for free, but the salary to be paid must be at least $50,000 a year. CEO Update also publishes a 28-page print list of jobs and sells subscriptions for its national registry of CEO-level jobs.

A thorough list of other exceptional general job boards and boards broken down by geographic region, issues area, or functional expertise can be found in the Resources section at the end of this book.

You can use most good job boards in two effective ways: actively or passively. Either way should provide you with ease of use, clear directions, and, most importantly, security and privacy.

Active Engagement

You can visit job boards as often as you'd like, entering your mission interests, functional expertise, and geographic desires, and discovering a listing of current jobs being advertised by employers. Some job boards add details about the organization and what it does. Others link directly to the organizations.

Another way to engage good job boards actively is to enter your résumé in an easy-to-read fashion. Such boards offer the employer paying to post the job the option of searching their résumé databases to find candidates. Some boards allow you to withhold identification information, and others allow you to approve who gets to see your résumé before the hiring manager is granted access.

Passive Engagement

One of the most useful features of good online job boards is getting a personalized e-mail delivered to your inbox on a daily or weekly basis. Once you have entered your requirements for your next job into their online forms, their systems identify posted jobs that meet your interests and send an e-mail directly to you. Surprisingly, for all the new advertising and outreach technology out there, some boards do this better than others.

Don't let the proliferation of Web-based job searching make finding a job harder rather than easier. If you find that you are overrun with jobs for which you hold no interest or are completely unqualified to fill, unsubscribe yourself from the e-mail service and go back to doing things the old-fashioned way, by manually searching the website each week. Further, if you find yourself getting lazy in your networking and relying on these e-mails as your only source of information about new jobs, unsubscribe at once and force yourself to work a little harder.

Online Networking Forums

The Internet has revolutionized job searching. Rather than dragging yourself to a monthly job-networking meeting in a damp public library basement, virtual networks have sprung up all over the world to provide quick and efficient methods of introductions, information transfers, and assistance requests. Sure, these groups still meet face to face at times, but now in a more targeted fashion, allowing you better to utilize your limited time.

Young Nonprofit Professionals Networks. YNPN promotes an efficient, viable, and inclusive nonprofit sector that supports the growth, learning, and development of young professionals. With 30,000 members at 30 chapters nationwide, YNPN engages and supports future nonprofit and community leaders through professional development, networking, and social opportunities designed for young people involved in the nonprofit community.

LinkedIn. LinkedIn is an online network of more than 330 million experienced professionals from over 200 countries around the world. Signing up, which is free, allows you to set up a profile, establish a complete digital résumé, and begin using the contacts of your friends and colleagues to meet their contacts of their friends and colleagues. Simply by reaching out to a contact and asking them to introduce you by e-mail to a contact they have, you can multiply your network quite rapidly.

Net Impact. Net Impact's mission is to improve the world by growing and strengthening a network of new leaders who are using the power of business to make a positive social, environmental, and economic impact. As alumni from MBA programs, these individuals are looking to use their business education for good. There are more than 120 chapters worldwide, a central office in San Francisco, and a flourishing online community.

Craigslist. A virtual version of the giant community bulletin board in your local supermarket, Craigslist.org now operates sites in most major cities worldwide, listing more than 500,000 new jobs each month and many more issue-related service and networking opportunities. It is a no-frills site, and its price tag reflects that: it is free to read and mostly free to post. But be warned: the aforementioned CareerXRoads survey learned that only 1.9 percent of hires were made over Craigslist in 2012.

Various Local Listservs. Listservs exist on every imaginable topic, and nonprofits are no exception. Doing just a little research, you can find listservs oriented towards, for example, Jewish philanthropy, gay fundraising professionals, or women in community development. There are also many listservs for nonprofits based on city, state or region. These listservs include messages on current regulations, funding availability, lobbying activities, networking events, training and technical assistance, and job announcements. Even just lurking (i.e., reading, not posting) to these listservs can serve as a "Nonprofits in Your Neighborhood 101" course. A more detailed listing of some of the larger listservs can be found at the end of this book.

Getting Headhunted: A Note about Nonprofit Executive Search Firms

Larger organizations that can afford to retain a nonprofit executive search firm to assist them often do so. A typical search firm will charge one third of the successful applicant's first year's cash compensation to perform this work. Some have minimum fees of anywhere from $25,000 to $60,000. While they seek nonprofit executives, the search firms themselves are mostly profit-seeking endeavors.

A search firm is only as good as the searches it has in-house at any given moment. As such, it does not pay to spend a great deal of time trying to get a headhunter to call you back. That said, many retained nonprofit executive search firms, just like their counterparts in the corporate sector, specialize in particular fields—from higher education, to health care, to advocacy—or functional areas of expertise, such as development, finance, or operations. If a firm doesn't have a search that is right for you presently, they may get something appropriate next month.

A great way to crack the executive search firm is to find a way to help them in a search where you are not a potential candidate. For example, if a search firm is representing a nonprofit with a job in finance, but you work in operations, call the headhunter and tell them about the people you know who might be appropriate or interested, or about the issue-related networking group you have joined where you could distribute the job announcement. Of course, once you have helped them, take a minute or two to mention your own job search. Note that you will send, along with the contact information of the individuals or groups you are recommending, your own résumé for their file. Because you have just helped them, they may be more open to hearing about your own search. Then, when you need to call them about the job you actually want, you can tell them that you "are Joe Smith, and as you'll recall, we talked about a search you did last month for . . . " Headhunters see hundreds of résumés each week. They are unlikely to search for your résumé when they get retained to fill your dream job, but they will remember that you talked and that you were helpful. With additional reminding, you'll be able to have your first directed conversation about your own skills and qualifications.

Many search firms are organized internally as individual profit centers. Recruiters may work together or operate their own individual businesses under the larger firm's umbrella, sharing overhead, staff support, and databases. Never assume, then, that if you know one headhunter at a firm, you know all of them or, more importantly, that they know you. Use your networking assistance accordingly. For example, you "are Joe Smith, and you talked last month with their colleague, Nancy Jones, about a job that was too finance related for you, but now you're excited to learn about the operations job they have just been retained to fill." Suddenly, you seem like a known quantity, someone who has already cracked the firm's armor. If you're in, you must have been approved by someone, right? Therefore, the headhunter may be predisposed to talk with you.

Unlike the corporate sector, there are no nonprofit executive search firms that represent job seekers as their agents. Some, though, like the (shameless plug coming . . .) Nonprofit Professionals Advisory Group (*www.nonprofitprofessionals.com*) are staffed with experienced headhunters who provide fee-based services to job seekers, like résumé consultation, interview training, or job search strategy development. Using these services is a good way to make sure that your corporate background is resonating with a recruiter in the nonprofit sector and that you are going about your search in the best possible way. A list of many nonprofit executive search firms can be found at the end of this book.

Getting Efficient: Career Fairs

Career fairs are a great opportunity for those with ten or fewer years of experience to approach a large group of nonprofit employers at once. Used well, these fairs can provide you with a quantum leap in your networking, because they give you direct, in-person, focused access to the right people at the right organizations.

These career fairs will, in some ways, resemble the career fairs you went to as you were seeking your first job out of college. There will be the same tables of employers with videos, brochures, job listings, and banners, and there will be the same overeager job seekers battling for their attention, except at nonprofit job fairs, at some tables, either or both the employer and/or the job seeker may be wearing a T-shirt and Birkenstocks instead of a three-piece suit.

By far, the biggest and most wide-ranging nonprofit career fairs are held by Idealist. They include the typical tables of employers but also attract organizations looking for volunteers or interns. In addition, Idealist now includes panels of experts providing valuable information on job searching or working in the nonprofit sector, and holds these fairs at college and graduate schools across the country.

What to Wear

Dress accordingly. Don't wear your blue pinstripe suit and leather wingtips. Normally, khakis and a button-down shirt will suffice for men and a skirt or pants and a sweater or blouse is fine for women. As with anything else, however, consider your audience. If you are looking for a job in a highly entrepreneurial nonprofit already friendly to MBAs, a suit may be better. If you are looking to move into a conservation group, that alligator-skin briefcase your grandmother gave you when you graduated from college might be a real turn-off.

What to Bring

You may be asked to set up an appointment for an interview, or quite likely you will be interviewed on the spot. Be prepared for either with your calendar, your résumé, and your compelling story about why you want to move into the nonprofit sector at this time in your life and career. Keep business cards handy, either from your current job or some that you have printed on your own from one of the many free outlets found online.

What to Do

Most career fairs advertise a list of nonprofits that have confirmed attendance as a way to attract job seekers and more nonprofits. This list is normally available ahead of time, with an updated list available at the door. Before charging up to the first table, review this list very carefully. Know who is there and whom you want to impress, and create a plan of attack.

Do not approach a nonprofit and ask it to "tell me about yourself." Technically the nonprofit is there to market the organization, but it is also there to fill specific positions. The staffers behind the table have been delivering their marketing pitch all day, and they may well be frustrated and tired. Research the nonprofit in question before you get to its table and ask directed, strategic questions that go beyond a basic understanding of who they are and what they do. They will be delighted to delve deeper with an educated, informed conversationalist. This approach will not only set you apart from other job seekers, it will show that you are taking this move into the nonprofit sector—and your desire to work for their nonprofit specifically—more seriously than your résumé alone might communicate.

Temporary Staffing Agencies

Temporary staffing agencies that expressly serve nonprofits have begun to spring up across the country. Like search firms, these agencies tend to be profit-seeking ventures. Most cover a functional area of expertise or a geographic area. Some examples include:

- **Professionals for Nonprofits.** Working in New York City and the greater Washington, D.C., area, Professionals for Nonprofits provides temporary, permanent, and consulting staff to nonprofits. **www.nonprofitstaffing.com**

- **Nonprofit Staffing Solutions.** Based in Washington, D.C., Nonprofit Staffing Solutions offers the opportunity to "Temp with a Purpose" to job seekers, while fulfilling the executive search, temporary, contract, and direct hire staffing needs of local nonprofit organizations. **www.nonprofittemps.com**

- **Accounting Management Solutions.** With both corporate and nonprofit placement arms, Boston-based Accounting Management Solutions offers temporary, permanent, and temp-to-perm opportunities for all types of financial positions, and this agency understands well how candidates can move between sectors. **www.amsolutions.net**

Gaining Experience: Putting More Than Just Your Foot in the Door

One of the best ways to immerse yourself immediately in a nonprofit network is to start working or volunteering for one. This can be as a one-time volunteer, a long-term volunteer, a consultant (paid or pro bono), a board member, an intern, or a temporary employee. We will cover later, in more detail, volunteering and board memberships as a way to improve your résumé and increase your knowledge. However, should you have time to begin working full-time or part-time in the nonprofit sector, there are avenues of assistance.

Internships, Temporary, and Temporary-to-Permanent Positions

For those just getting started, internships are an ideal way to get your foot in the door. Some are paid; some are not. Either way, you should design your internship to be like a real job, where expectations are clear on both sides. Tell your employer that you are looking to perform a very specific scope of work to learn or further hone a set of skills. In exchange, you would like assistance in networking in the nonprofit sector and a recommendation, if the employer feels comfortable, about the work you have performed.

Remember that many temporary jobs turn into permanent jobs. Others lead to permanent jobs with different responsibilities within the same nonprofit. While you are doing your assigned work, keep an eye out for other assignments that could showcase your broader skill set.

Just because you were hired to answer the phones doesn't mean you can't do other things, too. Treating your temporary position as if it were your dream job—answer every single call quickly and with gusto—will serve those less fortunate for whom the nonprofit exists, and it will be a shot in the arm for your job search. And, if you do it well, the nonprofit will be happy to give you more assignments.

Encore Careers for Baby Boomers and Early Retirees

There are 76.4 million Baby Boomers in the United States, and many of them are realizing that a retirement of nothing but golf and travel may sound like a dream come true at first, but only sustains them emotionally, mentally, and financially for so long. This is the generation that lived through Vietnam, the Civil Rights Movement, the Peace Corps, and the assassinations of John F. Kennedy, Robert F. Kennedy, and Martin Luther King Jr. They are the fastest-growing talent pool in the nonprofit sector and have a lifetime of righteousness, angst, and social justice stored deep inside, perfect for fueling their second career in the nonprofit sector.

The nonprofit sector is standing up and taking notice of the Baby Boomers. In fact, many nonprofits have been created to help ease these energetic, active, and interested professionals into a second career in the nonprofit sector. Encore.org (formerly Civic Ventures), a nonprofit based in San Francisco, is leading the charge. Its recent research has shown that Americans in the second half of life—regardless of income, educational level, or race—want to explore options for the next stage of life; retool skills, obtain new training, or pursue educational interests; use their skills and experience in flexible work or service opportunities; and make meaningful connections with their peers and their community.

The Next Chapter, an initiative of Encore.org, was created to provide expertise and assistance to community groups across the country that help people in the second half of life set a course, connect with peers, and find pathways to significant service. Local Next Chapter projects and related programs exist in dozens of communities nationwide and are growing every day.

In addition, other nonprofits, like Experience Corps and Senior Corps, have been founded with the express intent of providing significant volunteer experience with demonstrable results. Programs that provide long-term, direct service or opportunities where you can volunteer in central office administrative work are a good way of testing your mettle for this type of work, your dedication to the mission, and the level at which you'd like to do it.

Turning Networking into Consulting Assignments

Nonprofits often need high levels of support around major, organization-wide changes. These can include, but are certainly not limited to, executive searches, reorganization, training, or event management. At these times, nonprofits turn to consultants, individuals who can provide expertise without placing a heavy burden on the salary line of the budget. As nonprofits become more sophisticated, they are looking for consultants who can bring business expertise to their nonprofit world, and that is where you might come in.

Corporate career changers increasingly find themselves offered small consulting gigs to work on a specific project for a nonprofit while they complete their job search. Wonderful opportunities, these assignments allow career changers to get to know the nonprofit world from the inside out while getting paid a little something for their trouble. For example, a nonprofit needing assistance with creating a growth plan may want someone with the expertise to benchmark their competition's strategic decisions and how those decisions impacted their success. Or they may need someone to create accounting and bookkeeping systems as they set up a social enterprise venture in-house. The possibilities are endless, and job seekers who are creative can turn them into fruitful opportunities.

Getting Smart: Where to Learn More

Due to the legal and accounting requirements to retain nonprofit status, and because their donors demand it, the organizations you are targeting in your search are forced to be much more transparent than if you were looking for a job in the corporate sector. Getting information about nonprofits is relatively easy, and having it at your fingertips will impress your interviewers. Further information about specific nonprofits is available through a number of different avenues.

IRS Form 990

GuideStar's website *(www.guidestar.org)* includes a searchable database of more than 1.8 million nonprofit organizations in the United States and is the easiest place to find a nonprofit's tax return and audited financial statements. The "990," as it's simply known in the sector's lingo, lists the annual budget of the organization, its mission, address, revenue sources, highest paid consultants, equity, and expenses of the nonprofit, and can provide valuable insight to their financial sustainability. Nonprofits with revenue over $25,000 must file, although religious organizations and government entities are exempt.

Give.org

The Better Business Bureau's Wise Giving Alliance *(www.give.org)* provides charity evaluation reports as well as a National Charity Seal of Approval for charities that solicit contributions nationwide.

Annual Reports

Most nonprofits publish annual reports in some form or another. Larger nonprofits produce multicolor, multipage books and distribute them to thousands of stakeholders, donors, friends, and volunteers. Smaller nonprofits may have a two- or three-page version in a PDF file on their website. Regardless of their format, annual reports exist to tell donors how their money was spent in the prior year, what programs were run, who was served, and any exciting news about expansion of work over the past year or in years to come. They are both a description of the past and a road map for the future, and reading them before you interview will allow you to talk about how your strengths fit into this particular nonprofit and its needs, using its own language and focus.

The Nonprofit's Website

It may seem obvious, but many candidates never take the time to read the organization's website thoroughly. Not doing so is like writing a book report after renting the movie version. In fact, it is about the same as writing the report after dozing off during the movie's trailer. Reviewing the nonprofit's website is an essential part of developing your knowledge about the nonprofit, their programs, their people, and even their competition, as well as their technological savvy and the resources they have to put towards public relations and communications. Some websites even go so far as to list the biographies of the people you will be meeting; you can't get better prepared than knowing if you have something important, like an alma mater, in common with your interviewer.

Conferences and Seminars

Invest in attending conferences and seminars held by the leading lights in the nonprofit sector, whether they are on substantive topics, such as the latest trends in environmental programming, or on procedural points, like board training. Doing so will put you in a room with like-minded people who already are doing the jobs you would like to do. Plus, you will learn volumes of interesting, salient data to bring up in your networking and interviewing. These conferences vary widely, from the tactical to the ethereal; a good rule of thumb is that if you start rolling your eyes in the first 15 minutes, you are in the wrong place. Regroup, re-register, and try another conference.

Third-Party News Stories

Make sure to visit the websites of the sector's main newspapers and journals, such as the *Chronicle of Philanthropy*, the *Chronicle of Higher Education*, the *Nonprofit Times*, and the *Nonprofit Quarterly*. Do a Web search to see if any newsworthy items have been published recently about the organization. You may learn about scandals or crises, or about major grants and new projects. Either way, you will be more knowledgeable in your networking if you know the organization's public history.

Libraries

Often overlooked in this day and age of easily accessible Internet connections, the library is a terrific, free resource that should be utilized by all. Librarians know where to get any piece of information you can imagine, can put their fingers on databases and membership lists that are not accessible to the general public, and can point you in directions that will save you valuable time and resources. And, of course, libraries have Internet access, too.

Nonprofit FAQs

Finally, one of the best resources out there is Putnam Barber's overwhelmingly comprehensive Nonprofit FAQs. Hosted by the National Center for Charitable Statistics (*http://nccsdataweb. urban.org/PubApps/nonprofitfaq.php*) and begun in the early 1990s, this website acts as a veritable road map of the nonprofit sector's inner workings. Got a question about tax requirements? It's in here. Want to know what political activities are allowed by nonprofits? That's here. Looking to figure out how to get celebrities to help your nonprofit raise money? Yup, got that, too.

Conclusion

The best job search, nonprofit or corporate, is a targeted job search. Just as you once set your sights on your ideal job in the corporate sector, this chapter was intended to help you hone the direction of your nonprofit job search. Keeping in mind your whole history, including the jobs you've been paid to do and the ones for which you have volunteered your time, you should now have a clearer sense of yourself as a nonprofit job candidate.

Now that we have identified the entire three-dimensionality of your nonprofit candidacy through a self-assessment process, networking and informational interviews, and additional sector knowledge gathering, it's time to put together a résumé that will act as your chief marketing piece. In the next chapter, we will shape your past into a document that sells your future as a serious nonprofit job candidate. We'll address which sections, formats, and language to include and which to avoid. Where you may find yourself lacking, we will introduce resources that will help you fill in any gaps of knowledge, skills, or experience.

Testimonials from Successful Career Changers:

Bruce Trachtenberg, *Executive Director,*
The Communications Network, Naperville, Illinois

Bruce was serving as the public relations director for the Reader's Digest Association in the early 1990s. The company had just gone public, resulting in a windfall for the two private grant-making foundations created by the founders of Reader's Digest—DeWitt and Lila Wallace—who until then had held a majority of the stock in the company. Over the next couple of years, Bruce watched—and occasionally was asked to help out with some communications needs— as the DeWitt Wallace-Reader's Digest Fund and Lila Wallace-Reader's Digest Fund began to grow and establish themselves as major national grant-making organizations. "I'd been at Reader's Digest for more than ten years," Bruce explains, "and felt like my time at the company was nearing an end. I was ready for a move."

Around this time, the president of the two Wallace Foundations called Bruce and told him that the board had just approved plans for a major staff expansion to accommodate the growing assets of the foundation. One of the positions was for a communications director who would be responsible for starting an in-house operation; when the president asked Bruce is he knew of any good candidates, Bruce hesitated, hung up the phone, and after a few minutes of thought called back and said, "I know just the person for you. Me."

How did Bruce prepare himself to move into his nonprofit job?

"I didn't have a lot of time to prepare," says Bruce. So once he announced his intention to leave, he didn't waste time. Instead, Bruce did most of his learning on the job. "I spent lots of time in conversation with my colleagues, learning what they do and how I could help them," he explains. He also began making connections with as many people as he could who were outside the foundation but involved in philanthropy. One very helpful organization was called, back then, Communicators Network in Philanthropy. It was a volunteer group made up of people who held communications jobs at foundations whose primary reason for coming together was to network, exchange ideas, share best practices, explore common problems, and be available to lend a hand. Some 15 years later, that organization has evolved into The Communications Network, a stand-alone nonprofit that Bruce now leads as executive director.

How did Bruce go about finding his nonprofit jobs?

"The Wallace-Reader's Digest Funds job fell into my lap," says Bruce, "but I eventually left the foundation in 2000, drawn by the siren song of the dot-com sector and Worth. com." When the company started to teeter nine months later, Bruce began putting out feelers. A friend told him that the Edna McConnell Clark Foundation—a foundation he had long admired and whose past communications director he had respected—was looking for a communications director. Bruce dashed off a quick letter and a résumé, only to be told that the search was virtually closed—the foundation was only looking at candidates in case their finalist fell through. Still, he persevered, and it paid off. The finalist fell through, and Bruce, having impressed the recruiting firm and the search committee, was given the job.

Bruce's Key Lessons Learned:

- ✓ "Be prepared that things move more slowly in the nonprofit sector. Patience is a virtue."
- ✓ "The quality of a person's character and integrity matter as much as their skills and work experience."
- ✓ "After working in the nonprofit sector, 'settling' for a corporate position would have felt like a step backward."

Deborah Dinkelacker, *Executive Director,* VolunteerMatch, San Francisco, California

Deborah had a successful traditional corporate career. She studied political science at Yale University and got her MBA in finance at New York University. She worked in consumer packaged goods and then in consumer finance at PepsiCo and Colgate Palmolive. Deborah shifted into marketing at American Express in New York City, where she stayed for ten years and ultimately rose to be vice president for marketing of the consumer card group.

Deborah greatly enjoyed her time at American Express and, in fact, looks back on it with great fondness and deep appreciation. "My corporate experience helped shaped the leader and manager I have become," she explains. Yet Deborah recognized toward the end of her tenure that, while her financial satisfaction was quite high, her personal satisfaction was not. "I felt a remoteness from results," she says, "and at the same time, I began to develop an intellectual interest in, although not a personal passion for, mission-driven organizations."

What started out as intellectual curiosity has now developed into much, much more. "I began to feel a sense of injustice that nonprofits were somehow considered less worthy of excellent talent or the best new business thinking," she says. "While I knew that nonprofits had large numbers of excellent leaders, I felt that they still weren't getting their fair share of the talent and brain trust when forced to compete with corporates for employees." When it came time for her partner to take a job on the West Coast, Deborah moved too, shifting both her home and her career. Deborah took her first nonprofit position as the national director of marketing for membership services and donor development for the Sierra Club, but after a mediocre experience there, briefly went back to the corporate sector. When the opportunity arose at VolunteerMatch, she jumped at the chance to be its second president, following in the footsteps of a founder.

What made Deborah's first nonprofit experience harder than she expected?

Deborah didn't seek out enough advice before she made her move. "What I have since come to understand," she explains, "is that there is a tremendous amount of cultural diversity in the nonprofit world, and choosing the right nonprofit culture is essential to an employee's success, no matter where you were before." In looking for her second nonprofit, Deborah chose one more in line with her work personality. VolunteerMatch is a more analytical and information-oriented culture, and it exercises greater structure and discipline around decision making. Still, Deborah notes, "I had a lot to learn."

What was different the second time around for Deborah?

Sierra Club helped Deborah to understand what she needed to do: "Establish trust and establish credibility right away." Deborah's predecessor in her role at the Sierra Club had not been incredibly successful, and as a consequence, Deborah was greeted with skepticism. "I had never been hired into a position before where failure was expected by some, and I didn't take proactive measures to combat this self-fulfilling prophecy." When she got to VolunteerMatch, Deborah spent an enormous amount of time actively listening to her board members and staff, reflecting on how she was going to adapt her work style, and taking more time to explain her thought processes and secure consensus around decisions, even minor ones, because as she learned, "Few decisions in the nonprofit sector are minor."

Deborah's Key Lessons Learned:

- ✓ "Striking the right balance between the 'discussion' culture of the nonprofit sector and the 'action' culture of the corporate world can be hard. Action implies having to say yes to one option but no to several others, and turning down the option to help is difficult for most nonprofits to do."
- ✓ "You are not a savior. You have as much to learn from this nonprofit as it has to learn from you. Make sure you listen so that you don't miss it."
- ✓ "Instead of jumping right into a nonprofit job when the impulse strikes, spend a year volunteering either in a frontline, direct service role or as a board member to get a better understanding of the cultural diversity present in the nonprofit sector."

CHAPTER 2:
Building Your Nonprofit Résumé

When a headhunter or hiring manager advertises an open position, depending on the attractiveness of the job, between 100 and 300 applications may cross the manager's desk. On average, the hirer may spend about eight seconds looking at each—more likely, less.

Pretty scary, huh? If you can't capture someone's interest in those eight seconds, you can kiss your chances to interview for your fairy-tale job goodbye. So how do you create a résumé that tells your story accurately and effectively, conveys the logic behind your transition to the nonprofit sector, and grabs the headhunter's or hiring manager's attention so that you'll get a longer read?

Neon green paper isn't the answer, tempting as it may sound. Nor is presenting your résumé as you did for each of the corporate jobs you've held. This change in your career, like any change in direction, requires a shift in presentation, marketing materials, and spin. It may also mean gathering more experience with or intelligence about nonprofits and nonprofit management through one of many available board positions, volunteer or consulting opportunities, or educational programs. In short, you must internalize that this change requires the development and rollout of a whole new product line: the nonprofit you! This chapter will discuss the elements of the nonprofit résumé and how you can fill in any gaps.

Corporate Résumés Differ from Nonprofit Résumés

The nonprofit sector isn't about buzzwords or keywords. It's about relevance. The first thing most hiring managers look at when they open your résumé is your current job and your current company. This will most likely be the first strike against you. The second thing is your education; if it is solely business-related, it may be the second strike. Strike three may be a lack of numbers showing relevant scale or scope of your projects and accomplishments; a huge difference between what you've done and what you want to do, in either direction, won't make you look like a good fit for the position.

Rewriting your résumé to insulate yourself against these strikes is key. This section will walk you through each of the important parts of a résumé, showing you how to expand them, how to highlight relevant data, and how to reflect accurately your achievements. Then we will look at format types and appropriate introductions that present you favorably.

Size Matters

One of the most common questions professional résumé writers hear is, "How can I present a 15-, 20-, or 30-year career in just one page of text?" The answer: you cannot, and if you do, you have not given your career the marketing it deserves.

Feel free to elaborate to the length of two or three pages, if you have the material to do so. A four-page résumé from a 19-year-old college student internship applicant is obnoxious. Yet if you are at a level where you are comfortable applying for a senior executive position, then a one-page résumé does you a disservice, whether you are a sector switcher or not. While a recruiter will only spend a few moments looking at your résumé, you should provide enough material to communicate the full scope of your accomplishments. The recruiter will skip around to find the data needed to make a judgment about your candidacy. As such, length is less important than clarity of format and relevance of information presented.

A good rule of thumb is that you should have one page of a résumé for every ten years of experience. If you've been working for 25 years, you might have three pages to fill. If you've only been working for nine years, but have significant community volunteerism, you may be able to go to two pages and still have real content. If the résumé is getting too long but you still have significant publications, presentations, or other tangentially related work to include, keep yourself to a shorter résumé and include an addendum of selected materials.

Use Numbers

Let's go back to the imaginary hiring manager's desk stacked high with 300 résumés. Imagine further that each résumé is two pages and each cover letter is one page. That adds up to 900 pieces of paper. Throw in a few lists of references, reference letters, writing samples, or salary histories, and that quickly jumps to more than a thousand pieces of paper to muddle through. Knowing that at least 80 percent of these résumés are from unqualified candidates, the headhunter is going to speed through this pile.

The first thing most headhunters will look at is the résumé, not the cover letter. In fact, cover letter is hardly an accurate term, given that most hiring managers staple them to the back of the résumé. Most career changers fall back on their cover letter as the way to tell their story, but it's never seen because they have simply attached it to their old, irrelevant corporate résumé. (We discuss cover letters in more detail in Chapter 3.) Make sure your résumé tells your story—don't use the cover letter as a crutch. The résumé is, after all, what the headhunter sees first, only going back to read your cover letter if there is enough meat in your résumé.

Including specific numbers on your résumé allows a headhunter to quickly discern whether you have the required level of depth, breadth, and scope of experience for a particular position. Despite the fact that bottom-line numbers aren't the only things that affect the bottom line of a nonprofit, both the nonprofit and corporate sectors are data-driven. A headhunter may assume that if you have managed a budget of $200,000, you may be able to manage a budget of $500,000, or that if you've managed a budget of $5 million, you may be able to take the leap to $10 million. Yet the headhunter may also assume that if you have managed a budget of $200,000, you should take some steps between this and the $10 million corner-office job.

Specifically, list significant numerical data points that tell your story (e.g., revenue generated, alliances created, budgets reduced, staff managed, bottom-line growth, savings overall, speeches written, and press mentions secured). If you've done any nonprofit work or volunteer work, list numbers of dollars raised, staff managed, grants written, board members trained, and the like. But don't get too carried away. Listing number of marathons run, number and ages of children, or your own age is too much information, and it potentially provides some illegal material for the headhunter to consider.

Be Specific

When was the last time your day-to-day job reflected what that position description you agreed to years ago? If you are like most people, the answer is "not lately" or even "not ever."

Most of us fall into the habit of reproducing the bullet points of our job descriptions in our résumés, because it is the easiest starting point to explain what we do. However, your job description was probably poorly written to start with, and if you start with a poor outline, you'll end up with a worse résumé.

Your job description likely lists what you were supposed to do on a daily basis to fulfill the responsibilities of the job for which you were originally hired. It doesn't list your accomplishments—what you actually did—or how that work fit into the bigger picture of the corporation or organization. It certainly doesn't list all of the additional responsibilities you accumulated and for which you worked so hard. The nonprofit sector cares about the impact that you made in your corporate life.

Fleshing out a short bullet-point item into a longer description will make your achievement both more understandable and more interesting. Below are some examples of ineffective bullets and their longer, more successful rewrites.

Space waster:	Secured donations from private corporations.
Attention grabber:	Raised $5 million in corporate donations through three $1 million major gifts, four community events, and the recruitment of two new board members.

Space waster:	Managed staff and budget in accordance with company policies.
Attention grabber:	Spearheaded a staff of 12 and a budget of $1 million, managing both day-to-day operations and the development and implementation of a year-long, department-wide restructuring, which ultimately saved the company in excess of $200,000 per year.
Space waster:	Acted as public liaison for company for all external inquiries.
Attention grabber:	Led overall press strategy, weekly media outreach efforts, and the creation of collateral materials for a 14-partner coalition, resulting in coverage in print publications, including *The New York Times, The Wall Street Journal,* and the *Associated Press*, and on-air coverage in 843 radio and television stories.

Take Credit

The simple truth is that people don't always do what they were hired to do, and if they do, they don't often do it well. Your résumé should highlight not just what you did, but how the overall outcome was different because you were part of the process. Ask yourself, *What wouldn't have happened but for the fact that I was there?* If you were part of a team, highlight your role and make sure you acknowledge the team, but take appropriate credit for your contributions as well.

Most résumés do not take enough credit for the work done. A résumé is no time to be a shrinking violet; if you don't show off for yourself, the next candidate in the pile won't do it for you. As a corporate candidate for a nonprofit job, you'll have to be extra diligent about detailing how your accomplishments put you in good standing vis-à-vis the nonprofit's upcoming challenges.

Think of your résumé as talking points for your nonprofit hiring manager, most likely someone who doesn't understand where you have been or how, otherwise, to get the best story out of you during the interview. Rather than making them fumble through a foreign subject, spoon-feed them information in a way that allows them to understand where you have been and how your experience is relevant to their nonprofit. You can't do this without a bit of boasting; if you are especially shy or humble, putting this on paper makes it even easier, since the interview then becomes storytelling about "how" you accomplished your goals, rather than just taking credit for "what" they were.

Use Action Verbs

Verbs may take one of three distinct forms: occurrences (become, happen), states of being (are, seem, be) or actions (accomplish, strategize, bungee jump). Action verbs frame your experiences in terms of movement towards a goal and help you show off the results. Without action verbs, your résumé reads flat, and without a variety of them, your writing reads even flatter. Below are lists of action verbs appropriate for different types of skills you may list on your résumé.

Communications, Public Affairs, Public Relations, and Lobbying

acquainted	debated	framed	provoked
addressed	defined	handled	publicized
advocated	defused	influenced	quoted
affected	dispatched	informed	represented
aided	dispensed	interpreted	responded
aired	dissuaded	interviewed	reversed
answered	distinguished	introduced	spoke
apprised	educated	lobbied	sponsored
briefed	effected	localized	spread
cast	elaborated	marketed	targeted
communicated	elected	mobilized	taught
controlled	emphasized	narrated	testified
conveyed	expanded	persuaded	thanked
convinced	explained	phrased	translated
coordinated	exploited	profiled	transmitted
corresponded	fielded	promoted	

Creative

advertised	corrected	edited	printed
choreographed	crafted	exhibited	produced
chose	created	fabricated	published
circulated	criticized	fashioned	revealed
coauthored	critiqued	illuminated	showed
collaborated	customized	illustrated	simulated
collected	described	imagined	staged
composed	designed	improvised	substituted
condensed	detailed	modeled	tailored
conducted	displayed	named	traced
conserved	drafted	noticed	verbalized
contrived	drew	photographed	wrote
copied	duplicated		

Program Creation

adapted	devised	innovated	stimulated
added	devoted	orchestrated	submitted
admitted	diagnosed	originated	substantiated
adopted	diagrammed	pioneered	undertook
anticipated	directed	proposed	visited
chartered	established	reached	vitalized
commissioned	exceeded	reacted	volunteered
complied	experimented	safeguarded	won
conceived	founded	started	worked
conceptualized	inaugurated	steered	
demonstrated	initiated		

Project Management and Leadership

absorbed	deferred	invented	serviced
accelerated	delegated	kindled	settled
accomplished	designated	litigated	shaped
appointed	determined	managed	signed
approved	disciplined	motivated	simplified
authorized	drove	oversaw	solved
began	earned	praised	sparked
broadened	elevated	presided	spearheaded
built	employed	prevailed	specialized
catapulted	enforced	prioritized	specified
chaired	excelled	pursued	succeeded
completed	governed	ran	surpassed
conferred	granted	rewarded	terminated
consolidated	implemented	selected	thrived
constructed	instilled	sent	
consulted	instituted	served	

Evaluation and Assessment

actuated	endorsed	observed	reviewed
analyzed	evaluated	patterned	suggested
appraised	examined	penalized	summarized
assessed	exposed	perceived	surveyed
audited	gauged	predicted	tabulated
averted	graded	probed	tested
competed	indexed	processed	tracked
contrasted	inventoried	projected	validated
correlated	investigated	ranked	valued
disclosed	judged	rated	viewed
discounted	measured	realized	weighed
discovered	monitored	redesigned	

Organizational Development

achieved	diversified	lightened	staffed
acted	documented	organized	strategized
altered	doubled	performed	strengthened
amended	exchanged	permitted	stressed
augmented	excited	played	stretched
bargained	executed	preserved	superseded
challenged	finalized	protected	supervised
changed	focused	quadrupled	supplemented
channeled	formed	qualified	sustained
closed	headed	recruited	synchronized
committed	heightened	retained	synthesized
cut	hired	revised	trimmed
decided	induced	revitalized	tripled
decreased	inspired	revolutionized	witnessed
developed	led	stabilized	

Research and Analysis

applied	centralized	extracted	queried
ascertained	clarified	extrapolated	questioned
asked	classified	figured	read
assembled	cleared	hypothesized	requested
assigned	compiled	inferred	researched
assisted	concluded	inquired	searched
assumed	considered	located	speculated
authored	deduced	pinpointed	studied
carried	detected	polled	uncovered
cataloged	disproved	proved	unraveled
categorized	extended		

Data and Technical

automated	linked	planned	screened
checked	logged	programmed	segmented
combined	maintained	recorded	separated
compared	mapped	recovered	standardized
computed	minimized	reengineered	systematized
debugged	moved	repaired	updated
engineered	navigated	replacedreported	upgraded
entered	outlined	retrieved	used
isolated	overhauled	revamped	utilized
issued	phased	routed	verified
launched	placed		

Operations and Finance

acquired	functioned	opened	renegotiated
bought	furnished	operated	reorganized
budgeted	grouped	operationalized	restored
calculated	guaranteed	ordered	restructured
charted	guarded	paid	resulted
compounded	incorporated	priced	scheduled
contracted	incurred	procured	secured
counted	inspected	prompted	shopped
decentralized	installed	purchased	shortened
depreciated	instigated	quantified	shrank
divested	insured	reconciled	streamlined
estimated	integrated	reduced	structured
exempted	juggled	registered	supplied
fit	kept	regulated	supported
followed	licensed	rejected	tightened
forecasted	liquidated	related	transacted
formalized	merged	remedied	transferred
formulated	negotiated	remodeled	transformed
fulfilled	offset	rendered	

Capacity Building

activated	enabled	maximized	reshaped
advanced	encouraged	moderated	resolved
allocated	enhanced	modernized	salvaged
amplified	enlarged	modified	saved
awarded	explored	multiplied	took
balanced	familiarized	overcame	troubleshot
boosted	harnessed	participated	turned
brought	honed	practiced	unified
delighted	improved	prevented	united
dissembled	increased	rectified	
distributed	justified	refined	
eliminated	leveraged	regained	

Training and Technical Assistance

adhered	ensured	invested	prescribed
adjusted	exercised	lectured	presented
administered	expedited	mastered	provided
advised	facilitated	mediated	recommended
arbitrated	fortified	mentored	referred
arranged	guided	nurtured	rehabilitated
coached	helped	offered	reinforced
comforted	highlighted	oriented	reinstated
counseled	identified	passed	trained
disseminated	indoctrinated	prepared	tutored
engaged	instructed		

Fundraising, Community Relations, and Partnership Development

accessed	contributed	gave	raised
accompanied	converted	generated	received
approached	cooperated	greeted	recognized
attained	cultivated	grossed	sold
attended	delivered	hosted	solicited
attracted	eased	interested	tended
availed	elicited	interfaced	traded
borrowed	enlisted	invited	transported
called	enriched	involved	traveled
calmed	entertained	joined	treated
canvassed	financed	listened	welcomed
capitalized	fostered	merchandized	widened
captured	found	met	
catered	gained	netted	
contacted	gathered	obtained	

Use Appropriate Language

One of the biggest challenges you will face in telling your story is translating your corporate experience into nonprofit speak. Simply put, the languages of the sectors are different. The nonprofit sector has stakeholders, not shareholders; donors, not investors; clients, not customers. To ensure that the person reviewing your résumé understands that you can make this shift, begin by incorporating the language of the nonprofit sector into your résumé. The following chart will help you to see how corporate skills should be described on a nonprofit résumé.

Corporate employees . . .	Nonprofit employees . . .
. . . work for a company.	. . . work for an organization (or a cause).
. . . earn a profit.	. . . generate revenue.
. . . create an offering of stock or raise venture funding.	. . . solicit individuals for major gifts.
. . . achieve a return on investment.	. . . achieve impact from donated funds.
. . . sell a certain number of goods or services.	. . . serve a certain number of community members.
. . . make decisions that impact the bottom line.	. . . incorporate key organizational values into decisions.
. . . develop sales leads.	. . . research potential funders, stakeholders, and partners.
. . . create customer-focused marketing campaigns.	. . . advocate to impact social change.
. . . reduce governmental interference.	. . . capitalize on government grant opportunities.
. . . lobby for favorable policy change.	. . . educate stakeholders about effect of policies on issues.
. . . spearhead investor relations.	. . . achieve greater constituency buy-in.
. . . grow and develop customer base.	. . . manage and expand their constituency.
. . . rely upon staff.	. . . rely upon volunteers and champions.
. . . reduce tax liabilities for increased profits.	. . . balance budgets to retain tax-exempt status.

Like the corporate sector, the nonprofit sector lives and dies by the bottom line. Yet in the nonprofit sector, quarterly earnings reports don't exist. Not everything that impacts the bottom line can be accounted for on a spreadsheet. In fact, some nonprofit employees will attest that the most important things they do cannot be accounted for at all. This is, of course, heresy to a corporate honcho but the bread and butter of the nonprofit sector. Understanding this difference allows you to determine which accomplishments, skills, and knowledge you want to put forward on your résumé. After all, putting a specific brand of milk in every refrigerator nationwide is different than making sure every child has milk to drink at lunch. Communicating that you have internalized this difference is essential, and shifting your résumé from a traditional corporate résumé to one that can be read through a nonprofit lens is a great way to begin.

To get to know the language of the nonprofit sector, begin by reading it. *The Chronicle of Philanthropy (www.philanthropy.com)* is printed twice a month and is the major paper of those in the grant-seeking and grant-giving world. The *Nonprofit Times (www.nptimes.com)*, distributed monthly, covers the business side of the nonprofit sector. The *Nonprofit Quarterly (www. nonprofitquarterly.org)*, more of a journal, is printed four times a year with each edition focusing 80 or more pages on a particular topic of interest, and it often includes some of the best thinking happening in the sector today.

Tell the Truth

A 2014 Harris Poll survey on behalf of CareerBuilder found that 58 percent of employers have caught a lie on a résumé. More specifically, According to a 2003 survey by the Society of Human Resource Management, 44 percent of 2.6 million respondents said they had fabricated at least one thing on their résumé. A 2004 report by the Federal Bureau of Investigation estimated that 500,000 people listed college degrees they didn't have. Some misrepresent themselves by glossing over the truth, perhaps listing a job that lasted from December of 2011 to January of 2012 as "2011–2012" on their résumés. Others outright lie, boasting a fantasized degree or expertise or claiming credit for work they never did—and couldn't do even if given the chance.[2]

Nonprofits are stewards of public money and so have to answer to public scrutiny. Any good hiring manager or headhunter will run a credit, criminal, and educational check before extending an offer. If you lie, you will get caught. Worse yet, you won't ever be viewed favorably again by that headhunter, that search firm, or that hiring manager. The best bet is always honesty; remember, the nonprofit sector is made up of many people just like you who changed course midstream. Tell them your tale, and they might just understand where you're coming from.

Making Your Résumé Work with Skills from Your Corporate Career

A résumé is an opportunity to tell potential employers what you can do by showing them what you *have* done. This works well for those on a linear career path, where the next job is simply an increase in responsibility, scope, scale, or depth of current activities in the same general functional area or subject matter. For example, if you were looking to find a job selling commercial

---

2. http://www.money-zine.com/career-development/resume-writing/resume-fraud/

real estate in the greater Manhattan area, you would be well served by detailing what you have sold in Brooklyn in your current position. If you wanted to oversee brand marketing for an international corporation that sells luxury goods, you could bring forward your experience in brand marketing for an international corporation that sold high-end beauty products.

Nonprofit executives, hiring managers, and headhunters see too many résumés each day, however, to do the work for you, translating your experience in the corporate sector into their needs in the nonprofit sector. As you make this transition into the nonprofit sector, detailing your commercial coups or your marketing victories won't be good enough. To help the résumé reader understand how you can translate the past into the future, write your résumé not as a description of where you have been but, rather, as a selling piece about where you are going.

Think Strategically about Your Skill Set

Think about your career change to the nonprofit sector in terms of functional expertise rather than subject area expertise. Certain nonprofit jobs demand a deep knowledge of the issue area itself and the universe in which its funders operate. Others do not. Those that do not are easier for corporate types to get.

Most nonprofits divide their work between management, communications, operations, programs, and fundraising. Positions requiring programmatic expertise fall under the program area almost exclusively. To write grants; have in-depth conversations with funders; and develop, implement, and evaluate programs, for example, you will need expertise in the subject matter. A communications director can always learn enough to go five or six questions deep with reporters, but more likely the person in that role will be running press releases, copy for annual reports, or other announcements by the program expert before sending them to the printer. The communications director will land the interview chair on a local news program, but the program director will actually take the seat.

Corporate transitioners are more likely to find success by focusing on nonprofit jobs that demand only a functional (or line management) expertise, including a mastery of functional skills but only minimal knowledge of the mission of the nonprofit. These positions include administrative, finance, and operations functions and often make for the easiest career changes from the corporate sector. In most cases, these administrative, finance, and operations functions transfer smoothly across sectors: bookkeeping is bookkeeping and strategic planning is strategic planning. There are, however, some exceptions. Nonprofits are governed by a different set of tax principles, legal requirements, and public expectations. Accountants or lawyers looking to make the move should invest in additional education before claiming adequate expertise.

Let's look at a few examples of corporate types who transitioned by strategically transferring their skills from one sector to the other.

Rochelle, Customer Service Representative

Corporate. Rochelle is a customer service representative at a mortgage company. She interacts with external and internal customers, mortgage brokers, and account executives, providing information in response to inquiries about products and services and handling and resolving complaints.

Nonprofit. Rochelle would make an ideal nonprofit fundraiser or membership manager. Rochelle understands people and what gets them to yes. She has good listening skills and can be strategic in her timing in terms of what, when, and how she delivers information and asks for an investment in return.

Walter, IT Project Manager

Corporate. Walter works as an IT project manager in a health care company, planning, directing, and coordinating activities of designated e-commerce projects. He follows formal project methodology; develops plans and goals; and determines staffing, strategy, scheduling, budgets, and risk assessment to meet targets set out by shareholders and senior management.

Nonprofit. Like Rochelle, Walter has valuable skills to bring to the nonprofit sector. Nonprofit program directors use similar skills, providing leadership in developing program, organizational, and financial plans to fulfill the needs of donors, members, or community stakeholders. They look for ways to increase efficiency by incorporating the newest online resources and Web-based programming.

Leslie, Public Relations Executive

Corporate. Leslie is a public relations executive whose portfolio consists mainly of cosmetics companies. She manages all account operations, from writing high-profile news releases, pitching and placing stories, and planning media launches. In addition, she is in charge of developing new business and delivering sales pitches. To do this, she must be both excellent at the execution of public relations work and an expert on trends in her population segment.

Nonprofit. Leslie would be an attractive candidate to a women- and girls-focused organization in need of communications expertise or strategic corporate partnerships. Communications directors create, oversee, coordinate, and execute comprehensive communications and public relations plans, and they think strategically about positioning their organizations as leaders in their fields. In addition, they are often tasked with overseeing major corporate partnerships; Leslie's background would make her a credible face for the organization with such partners.

Skills That Transfer Well from the Corporate to the Nonprofit Sector

CompassPoint Nonprofit Services and the Meyer Foundation published *Daring to Lead 2006*, in which they surveyed nearly 2,000 nonprofit executives in eight cities about the future of executive leadership in nonprofit organizations.[3] Though nearly ten years old, their conclusions are still accurate in today's nonprofit job market. Among their conclusions, they found that

---

3. Compasspoint and Meyer Foundation, "Daring to Lead 2006: A National Study of Nonprofit Executive Leadership".

executives are placing new value on strategic planning, entrepreneurial concepts, and business development potential, because many of them do not have senior staff in charge of finance or development. In fact, their study showed that only 53 percent had a chief financial professional and 40 percent had a chief development professional. This held true for smaller organizations as well as others with more than 30 staff members.

Skills from the corporate sector are proving more and more transferable as nonprofits increasingly understand their value. In tandem, as the face of philanthropy changes, donors are becoming venture-focused, more hands-on, and exceptionally demanding of a return on their investment that maximizes capital, resources, and talent. To that end, nonprofits have opened up about what skills businesspeople can bring to the table.

Consider the following skills, identified by CompassPoint, which are essential for the nonprofit leader of today. You will have many of these on your corporate résumé.

Leadership and Influence

Corporations use financial incentives to get the best out of their employees. Most nonprofits do not have such a luxury. Instead, those in the nonprofit sector are challenged to influence their employees in other ways, by constantly connecting daily outcomes to overarching goals, underscoring the importance of personal contributions to the team effort, and encouraging employees to continue to work toward a solution to sometimes overwhelming problems. Solving world hunger doesn't happen in a day, a week, a month, or even a year, but achieving specific goals along the way allows nonprofits to benchmark their successes to being part of the ultimate solution.

Managing Up, Down, and Sideways

The nonprofit sector is made up of team contributions, not individual trailblazers. It is true that nonprofits are founded by dynamic, focused, charismatic superstars, but they are run on a daily basis by those who can ultimately manage well in all directions: up to the senior staff or board; down to the staff; and sideways to constituents, funders, and other stakeholders. Corporate employees who come out of a culture where contributions are recognized and an investment is made in personal growth will find the transition to the nonprofit sector less foreign. While the nonprofit sector is often limited by its ability to fund expensive employee training and exotic corporate retreats, it can allow staff to try exciting things and develop themselves into better contributors.

Delegating with Kindness and Empathy While Demanding Accountability

No one is in the nonprofit sector for the high salaries or fancy perks. Employees aren't motivated by climbing the ladder one more rung or scoring the bonus after closing the deal. They are there because they believe in the mission of the organization and need to feel that their contributions matter. Managers who delegate with this in mind will likely have the most productive staff.

Adaptability, Flexibility, and Openness in Management and Communications

There is no cookie-cutter type of person working in a nonprofit. Similarly, each of the various internal or external stakeholders you might encounter on a daily basis is different from the next. Those with a desire and demonstrated ability to work respectfully and comfortably with families, community partners, elected officials, donors, media, individual citizens, and other culturally and socioeconomically diverse groups will transition most easily to the nonprofit sector.

Ability to Manage a Broad Portfolio of Responsibilities

Because nonprofits are small—again, many have a budget of less than $1 million—they often pool jobs together. Not all nonprofits can afford a director of development and a director of communications and, instead, hire a director of external relations. Similarly, vice presidents of finance and operations abound. The type of work being done remains the same, but more is asked of each staff member.

Knowing How to Get to Yes

Salespeople spend their days researching potential customers, determining their needs and their timelines, and pouncing at an opportune moment. Nonprofits do the same thing, except with donors, not customers. Knowing when and how to ask for resources, embodying an organization's mission, and understanding human nature is key to any nonprofit executive's success.

Managing Dotted-Line Relationships

Nonprofits rely on the kindness of others to accomplish their missions. Whether it be a large monetary donation or hosted office space, free services like printing, or loaned executives, nonprofits must make nice with partners and stakeholders to whom they are indebted. In addition, many nonprofits collaborate with other organizations to accomplish their mission, like a neighborhood-wide cleanup or a statewide reading drive. These stakeholder relationships are dotted, not straight lines. Keeping these partners not only happy but deeply invested is a challenge, and skill at doing this is attractive to the nonprofit sector.

Delivering Impressive Returns

Nonprofit employees are asked to do more with less. A proven track record of delivering results where the resources are limited and time is short facilitates the sector switch. Public dollars come with public scrutiny, and private dollars come with private scrutiny, but scrutiny is scrutiny. The ability to withstand it, and perform well against it, is key.

A Long-Term View

Nonprofits do not judge themselves by quarterly earnings reports. Often, the pace of change is slower. Being able to see the big picture and manage any setbacks along the way with renewed energy and ideas is an important skill for a nonprofit sector employee.

A Distinct Passion for the Work of the Nonprofit

Working in a nonprofit setting can be difficult. Some days it can feel almost impossible. However, a genuine and deep passion for the work, as well as an intense respect and love of the people being served, can sustain even the most disheartened.

Chronological versus Functional: Which Résumé Format Is for You?

The purpose of a résumé is to land an interview. Nothing more, nothing less. It need not exclaim to a potential employer why they must hire you this instant. Rather, it should help you to get your foot in the door so that you can tell that story yourself.

Résumé formats come in all shapes and sizes. The most common formats—outside of the academic curriculum vitae—are chronological or functional. Determining which one is right for you is as easy as deciding where you have been and where you wish to go next.

Résumé Format

When deciding which format to use, ask yourself these questions:

- Are you looking to change sectors, careers, focuses, or industries?

- Have you switched jobs too often?

- Have you not switched jobs often enough?

- Is your résumé opening enough interview doors?

- Are you a first-time job seeker?

- Are you seeking a promotion within your organization or a more senior position within your field at another?

- Are you just returning to the workplace from maternity, family, or medical leave?

- Are you relocating?

- Have you just finished a graduate degree or additional education?

- Are you applying to a more conservative human resources director?

First Things Last: Chronological Résumés

The most common format is the chronological résumé. It presents your work history in reverse chronological order, starting with your current position and working its way back to the job you landed with that navy blue interview suit you bought during your junior year of college.

Chronological résumés are most appropriate for candidates with stable, solid career progression through one or, at most, two fields. If you started off your career as a circus performer, this is probably not the format for you. If your career path has been somewhat more linear, then this format can work well.

The chronological résumé highlights growth and maturity throughout an organization or career. It is the format employers see most often, and it provides them with an easy-to-follow structure for interviews. On its face, it looks like the simplest to prepare, but like all résumés, it's a toughie. It can also be poison for candidates crossing into new fields, leaping sectors, or returning to the workforce after an extended leave.

Putting Your Best Foot Forward: Functional Résumés

Functional résumés allow you to flaunt the skills of your choice and the experiences of which you are proudest. This format gives you the luxury of combining a lifelong dedication to community service with your corporate achievements when switching career tracks. It focuses attention on skills and achievements, rather than place of employment, which makes it ideal for midcareer changers or recent grads. As an added bonus, these résumés work well for candidates who want the world to forget about their brief professional dalliance with interpretive dance.

Lest you think this is the perfect format for you, beware. Many employers are immediately suspicious of these résumés, because they are often used to hide spotty employment records, long absences from the workforce, or inconsistent performance. Some employers just aren't interested in taking the time necessary to put together a complete picture of you and will discard functional résumés without a second look.

The Best of Both Worlds

A better option for candidates who want the advantages of both the chronological and the functional résumés (without any of the detriments) is to combine them into one, using a functional introduction to a chronological work history. With a steady hand and an excellent editor nearby, these combination résumés can prove to be the right solution for those who want to spin their career history into easily digestible sound bites while expounding on their track record in a familiar, easy-to-read format. Most importantly, the combination format allows experienced corporate employees to put their volunteer or board service up top, where it will be seen first.

The Nonprofit Résumé:
What to Include and What Not to Include

The corporate résumé reflects results; the nonprofit résumé reflects results and contexts. Nonprofit résumés reveal more about the individual and allow some personality to come through. Figures 2.1 and 2.2 show two résumés for the same position, one in the corporate world and the other for the nonprofit world.

The following nonprofit résumé sections reflect the "best of both worlds" format. It has an overview section, a chronological professional history, a listing of community involvement, education, and some various other sections you may wish to include. There is also a list of sections not to include.

Figure 2.1

Paula D. JobSeeker

62 Main Street
Omaha, NE 68106

email: paula.jobseeker@email.com
tel.: (m) 402-555-7708; (h) 402-555-4632

<u>SUMMARY</u>

Professional communications background with comprehensive writing, advisory, publicity and management expertise; particular experience in business, financial and consumer technology; international work and study experience.

<u>EMPLOYMENT</u>

Mainframe Computer Corporation (Omaha, NE)   **2004-present**
Director, Corporate Communications
- Wrote speeches, scripts and presentations for CEO and CTO.
- Managed internal and external communications of company news.
- Managed public relations activities, supervising a team to plan and execute media relations.
- Managed vendor relationships and budgets.

Smith Public Relations Worldwide (Omaha, NE)   1998-2004
PR Account Director
- Served as public relations executive, conducting communications campaigns to support clients in technology industry; trained, mentored and directed professional development of junior staff.
- Assessed clients' public perception and developed plans to define and promote their brands, launch their products and services, and raise awareness and credibility among key constituencies.

Smith Public Relations Worldwide (Omaha, NE)   2000-2001
Supervisor
- Wrote communication collateral including company overview and market background pieces, press releases, product/service profiles, and customer case studies for distribution to key audiences.
- Led media training, message development, and engagement booking for client spokespersons.

Smith Public Relations Worldwide (Omaha, NE)   1998-1999
Senior Account Executive
- Ghost wrote executive speeches, presentations and contributed articles, including business profile supplement for trade press and advertorial published in *BusinessWeek*.
- Edited and proofread all writing assignments produced by account teams for the clients.

Russian-U.S. Telephonica (Boston, MA)   1989-1998
Director and Founder
- Started consulting practice as U.S. agent to emerging Russian telecommunications provider.
- Taught seminars on emerging telecommunications technologies in both English and Russian.

Trade Resources USA (New York, NY)   1985-1989
Vice President
- Directed marketing and commerce initiatives for trade management and export consulting firm.
- Managed international purchasing projects including construction of colonial homes in Moscow, distribution of consumer electronics to retail outlets in Russia and supply of U.S. and European food and textiles to emerging privatized stores.
- Marketed U.S. and European high-technology products and services for export to the Soviet Union for international trading company.
- Oversaw contract fulfillment including distribution, delivery, implementation and training.

Polar Trading Limited (Rockville, MD)   1982-1985
Contracts Manager
- Marketed U.S. and European high-technology products and services for export to the Soviet Union.
- Oversaw contract fulfillment including distribution, delivery, implementation and training.
- Organized corporate exhibitions, designed marketing materials, developed client presentations.

<u>EDUCATION</u>

University of California, Berkeley Russian Studies major (BA 1982)

<u>SKILLS</u>
- Computer/technology proficiency: MS Word, Excel, PowerPoint, Internet
- Russian fluency: 10 years of academic study, extensive travel in Russia and business use of Russian
- Spanish proficiency: 11 years of academic study, including travel to Spain

Paula is applying for a job directing communications for a nonprofit that works with Russian orphanages to help improve conditions of the children living within them. This résumé, which she used for her last corporate job search won't get her the job. Let's see why:

Paula is relying too much on her job description to show what she is supposed to be doing. Nothing here shows the reader what she has accomplished.

This section worries the reader that Paula has jumped around a lot, when a closer inspection shows that she has had promotions within the same company.

None of these jobs make it clear to the reader why she would be qualified for the nonprofit sector.

Of course Paula knows how to use these basic computer programs. Listing this, and listing it under "Skills" hides the deep linguistic background she has.

Figure 2.2

Paula D. JobSeeker
62 Main Street
Omaha, NE 68106
email: paula.jobseeker@email.com
tel.: (m) 402-555-7708; (h) 402-555-4632

Paula expanded her résumé to two pages and added in much of the volunteer work she has done over the years, thereby framing her background as directly applicable to the nonprofit sector.

Note how much more broadly Paula describes herself in this summary. Instead of writing a description of her current corporate self or for profit job, she describes her whole self, and pitches herself for the job she wants to have.

SELECTED CAREER HIGHLIGHTS

A seasoned external relations executive with a background in nonprofit, education, and corporate communications. Fluent in Russian and Spanish, and with comprehensive writing, advisory, publicity and leadership expertise; experience managing relationships with senior executives, media, and external community; extensive track record in school admissions as communications liaison between college, alumni, and prospective students; international work and study experience. Selected accomplishments include:

This highlights section brings Paula's paid and volunteer work right up front where the reader can see it.

Here's where Paula really spoon feeds her corporate and volunteer work to her reader.

- **Marketing & Public Relations:** Created marketing public relations campaigns for corporations and nonprofits, both internationally and domestically, which increased awareness and raised capital, funds, and memberships.
- **Event Management:** Managed more than 50 events for local nonprofits, institutions of higher education, and *Fortune 50* CEOs and their shareholders. Events ranged from black-tie fundraising dinners to small meet-and-greet affairs.
- **Strategic Communications:** Developed strategic communications plans internally and externally, in coporations with offices around the globe, and locally for the Boys and Girls Clubs of Omaha.
- **Operational and Team Management:** Participated in agency operations and communications meetings to assess, plan and execute strategic objectives to ensure that best practices and highest quality standards were implemented agency-wide.
- **Fundraising and Partnership Development**: Successfully raised $130,00 on behalf of the Boys and Girls Clubs of Omaha, and developed more than $10M in new business development internationally for Smith Public Relations.

A little name drop here to make sure there is some concrete nonprofit work upfront is always a nice tough.

EMPLOYMENT

Mainframe Computer Corporation (Omaha, NE)   **2004-present**
Director, Corporate Communications

Note how these four bullets say so much more about people than profits than the four bullets on Paula's corporate résumé.

- Developed and implemented communications initiatives which increased awareness of this global, public software company and led to financial and industry success. Wrote and delivered speeches, scripts and presentations for CEO and CTO which educated and built confidence among customers and shareholders.
- Developed relationships with investor community, managing external communications of company news through press releases, website, conferences, quarterly and annual earnings reports, and investor tours. Oversaw 16 public relations activities per year attended by upwards of 25,000 shareholders.
- Raised employee morale and reduced staff turnover by aggressively increasing internal communications including development of letters from the CEO, internal news announcements and employee newsletter.
- Managed more than 20 vendor relationships and budgets for corporate events, collateral production and investor and public relations activities.

Each of Paula's bullets not show that the work she did was in pursuit of a greater mission, and not just task-oriented.

Bullets like this not only show results, but results that are focused on profits, but also people. Paula did her job, but she cared about the staff along the way.

Smith Public Relations (Omaha, NE)   **1998-2004**
PR Account Director (Mar'02-Feb'04); Supervisor (June'00-Mar'02); Senior Account Executive (June'99 -June '00)

- Served as public relations executive to a $10M portfolio of clients, including start ups, public companies, global enterprises, and nonprofits. Selected clients include: MCI WorldCom Advanced Networks, Project Oxygen, System Software Associates, UUNet, Vanguard Managed Solutions. Boys and Girls Clubs, and the Junior League.
- Ghost wrote executive speeches, presentations and contributed articles, including business profile supplement for Gartner report and advertorial published in *BusinessWeek*. Edited and proofread all writing assignments produced by account teams for the clients.
- Created growth opportunities for junior staff, led account team performance reviews and mentored three account executives. Designed team project for interns, providing coaching and feedback. Hired two interns as FT employees.
- Wrote communication collateral including company overview and market background pieces, press releases, product/service profiles, and customer case studies for distribution to key audiences.
- Led media training and message development workshops for client spokespersons and arranged speaking engagements at trade shows and conferences.

Paula combined these jobs to show stick-to-itiveness and upward mobility. She also added a section on the great breadth and depth of her client portfolio, even dropping the names of a couple of nonprofits with whom she worked, even though they were limited engagements.

COMMUNITY LEADERSHIP AND VOLUNTEER WORK

University of California, Berkeley College Alumni Volunteer Chairperson   **(1998-present)**

Recruit alumni and lead volunteers in support of the off campus admissions efforts. Direct the program for the Omaha area, coordinating with alumni community to interview prospects and participate in college fairs. Serve as liaison between Admissions Office staff and alumni community to promote the College, oversee the interview and evaluation process, and ensure representation in area events. Plan and participate twice annual regional information workshops for prospects and receptions for accepted applicants.

- University of California, Berkeley Alumni Admissions Volunteer (1989-present)
- Conduct off-campus interviews with and write evaluations of high school applicants.
- Boys Club of New York Mentor (3 years)
- Coached group of 15 pre-teens in academic and recreation activities at Harlem Boys Club facility. Successfully raised $130,000 from corporation sponsors and individual donors to build a new playground structure.

ADDITIONAL EMPLOYMENT EXPERIENCE

Russian-U.S. Telephonica (Boston, MA)   **1996-1998**

Director and Founder

- Started consulting practice as U.S. agent to emerging Russian telecommunications provider.
- Developed and managed strategic partnerships between U.S. and Russian equipment manufacturers, service providers and international distributors, establishing channel partnership for Motorola.
- Participated in seminars and conferences worldwide to assess emerging technologies and industry trends.
- Taught seminars on emerging telecommunications technologies in both English and Russian.

Trade Resources USA (New York, NY)   **1993-1996**

Vice President

- Directed marketing and commerce initiatives for trade management and export consulting firm.
- Managed international purchasing projects including construction of colonial homes in Moscow, distribution of consumer electronics to various retail outlets in Russia and supply of U.S. and European food and textiles to emerging privatized stores.

Polar Trading Limited (Rockville, MD and Moscow, Russia)   **1989-1993**

Contracts Manager

- Marketed U.S. and European high-technology products and services for export to the Soviet Union.
- Oversaw contract fulfillment including distribution, delivery, implementation and training.
- Organized corporate exhibitions, designed marketing materials, developed presentations of client
- products and technologies to prospective buyers.

EDUCATION

- **University of California, Berkeley** Russian Studies major (BA 1982)
- **Moscow Energy Institute,** Russia Chosen by the American Council of Teachers of Russian for semester study and training program (Spring 1988)
- **Georgetown University** Political and Economic Russian: specialized language study (1992)
- **Yale University** Summer immersion program in advanced Russian (1987)

LANGUAGES

- **Russian fluency:** 10 years of academic study including semester in Moscow; 16 subsequent years of professional use of Russian with business associates, including multiple trips to Russia
- **Spanish proficiency:** 11 years of academic study, including travel to Spain

REFERENCES

Andrei Vladovsky, Board President, Russian-American Sister City Program, Omaha Affiliate, (402) 555-9756.

Jack Williams, Executive Director, Boys Club of New York, (212) 555-4752

Beatrice Derkach, Chief Communications Officer, Multicultural Alliance of Nebraska, (402) 555-8631

Overview/Professional Achievements

Overview sections in traditional corporate résumés list currently popular corporate-speak keywords targeted at computer scanning software. Nonprofit résumés don't need these words. For starters, most nonprofits can't afford this software. Further, corporate-speak isn't relevant. Listing your "P&L management" or "strategic mergers and acquisitions" or "global market identification" experience shows that you haven't internalized this sector change and that your transition may be bumpy. It screams to the hiring manager, "Proceed with caution!"

A better strategy is to use the "best of both worlds" résumé and write an introduction to yourself that brings together both your paid corporate work and your unpaid community service or professional leadership. The reader may still look at your current employment and job title but will do so through the lens of the skill set you are putting forward.

Change the title of the section from the vague "Overview," "Summary," or "Background" to something more action oriented like "Selected Career Highlights" or "Professional Achievements." This lets the reader know that you are actually putting forward a track record here, not a laundry list of management-speak, buzzwords, and fluff. Even if you talk mostly about the last four volunteer positions you held, you are still detailing the professional skills you bring to the table. Whether you got paid for the work or not, your experiences are still strengths and should be treated as such.

Because it is a summary of the entire document, you may want to consider writing this section of the résumé last. Once you have sorted out the rest of your résumé, this section becomes a longer version of your elevator speech. Start with a general statement about yourself and move into the details in full nonprofit-speak. Here are some examples of successful overview first sentences:

- **Example #1.** "A seasoned professional with more than ten years of experience managing high-level corporate activities and mission-driven nonprofit volunteer programs. Selected accomplishments include . . . "

- **Example #2.** "Dual JD/MBA with a track record of excellence within nonprofit and corporate environments. Career highlights include . . . "

- **Example #3.** "An up-and-coming star looking to dedicate energy, education, and experience to making a difference in the nonprofit sector. Initial successes include . . . "

Professional Experience

Your professional history outlines the paid jobs that you have held. It includes company name, title, location, and dates of service in the heading section, followed by details about accomplishments and achievement. For ease of reading, it is generally presented in bullet form rather than paragraph form. Because the nonprofit reader of your résumé may not know each of the businesses for which you've worked, you may also wish to include a sentence or two about the company's size, history, and focus.

This section should be written in reverse chronological order. Start with the most recent job and work your way back. Unless it is relevant to this job search, you don't need to go all the way back to the very first job you held 20 years ago.

Handling Current Unemployment

If you are unemployed, consider this a grand opportunity to "employ" yourself in the nonprofit sector, volunteering in an administrative or operational function (e.g., not just tutoring children but helping to run the tutoring program by creating and implementing a volunteer recruitment effort) or doing pro bono consulting for a nonprofit or two—or seven—of your choice. It's an excellent way to show dedication to the sector and, at the same time, have the first job on your résumé not read as "Corporate America." It is as easy as listing your new volunteer work as if it were your current job, assuming that you spend at last 20 hours a week at it, or creating your consulting firm of "Joe Smith Consulting" and bullet pointing actual assignments and projects as if they were paying clients. You should, of course, never lie about the status of this work, but it's perfectly fine to be spending 40 hours a week or more "working," even if it is unpaid.

Community Involvement

In the typical corporate résumé, the community involvement section is almost an afterthought. There is usually only a line or two dedicated to the most current charitable activities. At most, it lists just the name of the organization and perhaps the title held, be it volunteer or board chair.

For the nonprofit résumé, consider this section a "Part B" to the "Professional Experience" section above it. Like the skills you gathered in the corporate sector, the lessons learned in the nonprofit sector are arrows in your professional quiver. You have been drawing upon each in your corporate life and will continue to do so in your nonprofit life. Not listing this work, then, only tells half of your professional story.

Education

Like your professional history, education should be listed in reverse chronological order. Be sure to include the institution of higher education, your degree and major, as well as the date of graduation or years attended if you did not graduate. If you have gone through any additional continuing education that is relevant to this job search and better prepares you for the sector switch, list it here, too.

Grade Point Averages

Any honors, scholarships, impressive internships, or awards should be listed under the institutions at which they were awarded. Do not list your grade point average (GPA), even if it was a 4.0. You *can* say magna cum laude, cum laude, or Phi Beta Kappa, which communicates the point that you were a cut above the other students. At any other level, you risk additional and unnecessary judgment. Remember when you brought home a 98 in third grade spelling and your dad asked where the other two points went? Nonprofits put high stakes on education and are often a bit snobby about it.

The exception to this rule is the "bootstrapping loophole": if you worked full-time while putting yourself through school and are exceptionally proud of your less-than-perfect but still impressive final GPA, make sure you note under your education that you "completed all class work while carrying both a full-time course load and working 40 hours per week to pay tuition." It's a nice story, and you should get credit for it.

Handling Ageism

Ageism is illegal, but everyone who looks at a résumé calculates age from the date of graduation. It might seem logical, then, to remove your date of graduation, but do so at your own risk. Whether or not you list your age, the hiring manager is still eventually going to meet you face-to-face. The best plastic surgeons in the world might not be able to make a young, gritty nonprofit staffed with 27-year-olds appreciate a 65-year-old corporate retiree; some might recognize the importance of "gray hair" for credibility and wisdom, but others won't. Instead of wasting their time and yours, be up front about your age at the start.

Additional Sections That May Be Relevant

Depending on your particular career history, there may be some additional sections that you want to include. For most, the details under each section are likely to fit into the basic sections already discussed. For others, however, it may be important to give more information.

Publications and Presentations

Publications and presentations are an ideal way to show subject matter expertise in a particular programmatic area. If your résumé is getting too long, consider writing a basic résumé with an addendum of "Selected Publications and Presentations." This approach will allow you to send in a short, focused résumé but also include the extra meat needed to make your case strongly.

Professional Affiliations

If you have professional affiliations, such as membership in the Association of Black Accountants, Home Decorators of America, or Society for Human Resource Management, list them here. If, in addition, you also have community involvement, such as in Kiwanis International, a parent-teacher association, or a neighborhood watch program, consider combining these sections under "Professional Affiliations and Community Leadership." This detailed affiliations and associations section will not only make your résumé less of a laundry list, it will also guide the eye to the important nonprofit work you have done.

Licensure and Certification

List any specific licensure or certification you have that is relevant to the job for which you are applying. For example, your bar membership always matters, but your certification as a real estate agent may not. Don't let yourself look as though you are all over the map (i.e., tried this, tried that, and now on to the nonprofit sector for career number seven).

Awards

Most awards you have received should fit into your professional chronology. For example, if you were awarded "Employee of the Month" six times running, that should be listed under the job where you received the accolade and even reference the work that led to such recognition. Awards for things not related to paid or unpaid professional achievements, like a softball championship, are entirely irrelevant in a résumé and may distract your reader.

Computer Skills

A hiring manager will assume that, in this day and age, you know how to use word processing and spreadsheet development software like Microsoft Word or Microsoft Excel, know how to perform basic research tasks on the Internet using any number of browsers, and have more than a passing understanding of Windows or Mac platforms. Stating that you are skilled at Microsoft Word is about as relevant as stating that you can read.

Some jobs require technology skills above and beyond basic computer functionality. These include fundraising software, presentation software, programming, or coding for the Internet. If you are applying for a job that requires such skills and you are comfortable using the computer program in question, list it on your résumé or in your cover letter. If not, don't list your computer expertise at all.

Technology and Ageism

Another reason some choose to list their computer expertise is because they feel they may be suffering from ageism and want to show that they aren't a relic when it comes to modern technology. By all means, if you are at all concerned about ageism, certainly don't list this technology to protect yourself from it. It will only serve to heighten any concern about whether you can keep up, get your hands dirty, or are current with the newest technologies if you seem defensive at all. Instead, let the rest of your great and active work speak for itself.

Sections to Avoid on Your Nonprofit Résumé

In all cases, use the doctrine of relevance to determine what belongs or does not belong on a résumé. Just because the nonprofit sector wants to get to know more of your personal side doesn't mean they want to see it in your résumé. Put less relevant facts, like your junior high school project saving cats, feeding the homeless, or joining the Girl Scouts, in the cover letter if they add some important dimension to your application, or bring them up in an interview if they don't impact your credentials but will help determine your personal fit. And you can always keep them to yourself.

Your reader is already spending a limited amount of time on your résumé. If you fill that time with irrelevant, confusing, or disturbing data, you've not spent your time wisely. Instead of distracting them, leave out the following sections so they can focus on learning about your relevant achievements.

Objective

The "Objective" is a waste of space on your résumé: your objective is to get the job for which you've just applied. If a hiring manager is reading your résumé, then your objective is already apparent. Plus, if poorly written, it's the death knell of your career change. Saying that you want to find a job that uses your skills and provides you with career advancement is off-putting; the hiring manager doesn't want to know what the organization will do for you but what you will do for the organization.

Personal Interests

Listings of personal interests can be a wonderful way of showing who you are, rather than *what* you are. You may be a stockbroker by day but a budding chef at night. Telling a recruiter that you are interested in "conversation," scuba diving, martial arts, marathon training, or juggling is interesting but possibly not relevant. If as a budding stockbroker, you want to get a job investing the endowment of a cooking school, that's another story. But be conscious of the message your personal interests might send: if you graduated on a needs-based scholarship from Yale and then were invited, all expenses paid, by your roommate's family on her graduation trip around the world, the combination of "Yale" and "world traveler" might paint a very different picture for your résumé reader than what you know to be reality.

Pictures

Do not include pictures on, or attached to, your résumé. It makes you look less serious and it incapacitates the résumé reader from being able to make a judgment about you based on your skills and your experience rather than your looks.

Health, Age, Marital Status, Children

It is not only irrelevant but actually illegal for a hiring manager to take into consideration your health, age, or marital status or the number of children, dogs, cats, birds, or monkeys you may have. Do not include this type of information in your résumé or cover letter. Disclosing that you are an "active, healthy, 57-year-old man" just worries them that you might not always have been active and healthy, or that you are threatening to sue for age discrimination if they don't hire you. Why play with fire? Again, let your accomplishments speak for themselves.

Handling Diversity

Federal and some state laws protect job candidates and employees from discrimination if they fall into a protected class. Protected classes include race, color, religion, creed, sex, nationality, age, disability, veteran status, and sexual orientation. Everyone belongs to at least one protected class; for example, you cannot be denied a job simply because you are a man or a woman.

One of the major differences between the corporate world and the nonprofit world is that the nonprofit world not only wants to know what makes you different, but it will likely celebrate you for it. Your approach comes down to a question of personal comfort about putting your full self out there. If your extracurricular activities include memberships in, for example, the National Association of Asian American Professionals, the National Society of Hispanic MBAs, or the National Coalition of 100 Black Women, and you feel comfortable that the hiring manager knows your race from your paper application alone, make sure you list that information. Similarly, nonprofit employers are unlikely to bat an eyelash at job seekers who are members of the National Gay and Lesbian Law Association, the Jewish Community Center, or the American Gulf War Veterans Association.

It is by no means necessary that you list these things, but keep in mind that many nonprofits score big with funders, community members, and the media if they can show that they not only have a highly qualified staff but a diverse one, too, that represents the community they serve.

A Note on Political Correctness

Nonprofits, depending on their particular focus, tend to be politically correct to the extreme. There may be some cases where you opt not to include certain activities based on the particular focus of the nonprofit in question. For example, several years ago, the Boy Scouts of America got into some legal trouble for not allowing openly gay males become scouts or leaders. Most local chapters had nothing to do with this choice, and many rallied against it. However, if you are applying to an organization that works on behalf of civil rights and you lead your local Boy Scout troop, you may want to proceed with caution, lest you be judged unfairly as part of the problem. Instead of putting this activity on your résumé, if it was a watershed moment for you, shape your cover letter around it.

Steps You Can Take to Improve Your New Nonprofit Résumé

Now that you have begun to craft your résumé, you may have noticed that some pieces are missing. When looking at career changers, most hiring managers are looking for some sort of commitment to the sector leap. Does your résumé have this?

Showing a track record of forethought may be as easy as incorporating your current and past board work, community leadership, or relevant education on your résumé. For others, changing sectors is an ideal opportunity to get involved in new ways with issues about which you have passion—human rights, animals, equal representation, the environment—or with community organizations to which you are already tethered—a child's school, an institution of higher education you attended, a place of worship, or a political campaign, to name just a few. This career move is a perfect time to build a skill set through continuing education around a new career path, either enhancing what you already know or developing in a whole new direction. The experience and exposure you gain through board and volunteer work and continued education gives you both a growing network with which you can start your job search and the credibility to do it well, not to mention the perfect résumé bullet points.

Get on Board: Discover What You Can Do as a Board Member

Nonprofit boards are similar to corporate boards in many ways. They each provide oversight for a legal entity that has been incorporated with either a state or national government. They often recruit socially or strategically, depending on their size, history, and growth trajectories. Their sizes range from just a few members to a cast of dozens. The major difference is that nonprofit board directors do not receive any compensation for their service. Let's talk about why you should join a board and how you might go about doing so.

What Can You Do for the Board?

Board members in the nonprofit sector are expected to fulfill the basic duties as outlined in the "Ten Basic Responsibilities of Nonprofit Boards." Above and beyond that, however, smart nonprofits grow their board strategically instead of socially. If you are invited to join a board, it is likely that you appealed to the chair as someone who could provide insight or energy around a current or planned initiative, whether that be a volunteer recognition event, a fundraising campaign, or a strategic planning process.

Whether explicitly stated or not, most boards today still work with the "4G" model: Give, Get, Govern, or Get Off.

Ten Basic Responsibilities of Nonprofit Boards[4]

1. Determine the organization's mission and purposes.

2. Select the chief executive.

3. Support the chief executive and assess that person's performance.

4. Ensure effective organizational planning.

5. Ensure adequate resources.

6. Manage resources effectively.

7. Determine, monitor, and strengthen the organization's programs and services.

8. Enhance the organization's public standing.

9. Ensure legal and ethical integrity and maintain accountability.

10. Recruit and orient new board members and assess board performance.

Give (Financial Investment)

You will be expected to provide a financial donation; many nonprofits leave this to your discretion, but some phrase their expectations in such terms as, "Give an amount that reflects your commitment to the cause," or, "Please have this be the top philanthropic gift you'll make this year." Don't be disheartened by the financial aspect of board service. Remember, if all ten board members each give $5, this commitment of 100 percent shows an investment on behalf of the board much greater than if only 20 percent of the members gave a total of $50.

Get (Friend Investment)

You will be expected to become a public champion of the cause, putting your name on the organization's letterhead and your friends and colleagues in their outreach database. At fundraising events, you might be expected to buy a table and sell tickets to your friends to foot that bill. When in-kind corporate donations, like computers or printing, are necessary, the nonprofit may look to your place of work as a resource. As the organization needs spokespeople, to gloat about successes or defend a crisis, they may look to you.

Govern (Time and Knowledge Investment)

You will be expected to provide your time. Attendance at 75 percent of meetings is customary, so make sure you know when meetings are held so you can rearrange your schedule to attend. There likely will be at least one annual full-day (or longer) planning retreat and other volunteer

---

4. Richard T. Ingram, T*en Basic Responsibilities of Nonprofit Boards,* (BoardSource, Washington, D.C.: 2003). This is an excellent resource for those interested in learning more about what nonprofit board service entails.

events throughout the year that you must attend. In addition, you will be expected to serve on at least one of the standing committees, usually governance, fundraising, communications, human resources, evaluation, program, or finance. Then there are ad hoc committees that exist for a sole purpose and have a beginning and an end. These committees can include, but are not limited to, audit, search, events, strategic planning, and fundraising campaigns.

Get Off (Stepping Down or Sideways)

If you aren't quite ready to fulfill all the commitments of a board, choose to serve on an advisory council of an organization you enjoy. In some of the largest nonprofits, advisory councils exist as a group of impressive names that lend credibility or fundraising capacity to a nonprofit. In most smaller nonprofits—meaning most nonprofits—the advisory council can be a breeding ground for future board members, or it can be an off-ramp for board members who are no longer at their peak of service. In these nonprofits, advisory council seats usually come with a smaller expected financial commitment but with specific committee tasks and workload expectations. For example, you may be assigned to the technology committee to redesign the nonprofit's website, or to the strategic planning committee for a one-time benchmarking project or to determine whether a revenue-generating enterprise is feasible.

Which Board Is Right for You?

Before you get yourself on a board, make sure it is the right board for you. Determining which board is right for you requires an honest assessment of your skills and interests as well as an understanding of what you can give.

Where is your passion?

Just as you dissected the vast nonprofit sector to find the organizations that interested you, start by narrowing down the universe of nonprofits to boards you would like to join.

What kind of organization brings out your best?

While the list of issue areas in the nonprofit sector is vast, the types of nonprofit boards are not. There are, essentially, four types of nonprofit boards: founding boards, working boards, governing board, and fundraising boards. Depending on where they are in their lifecycle, nonprofits will have one or some combination of these four types of boards.

What Can the Board Do for You?

Let's talk about the obvious benefits you would enjoy if you were to join a board. First, the board oversees an organization whose mission is close to your heart. Second, the board will allow you to play a role you enjoy. Third, the board has expectations and needs around giving, getting, and governing that you can meet. But most importantly for you, the board will help you find a job in the nonprofit sector!

Your time, energy, intelligence, and financial resources—or connections to such—are worth something. Think strategically about what the board can do for you. In return for what you will be giving, you should be clear with yourself and others about what you are expecting in return. Use the board to build your knowledge of the nonprofit sector, a particular mission area, or a skill set, but also use it as a platform to show influential people in the nonprofit world your expertise and competence.

Skill Building

Have you always been interested in animals and recently learned of the fascinating research being done in zoos across the country? Have social or business connections to those in the food industry? Never planned an event or done any traditional nonprofit fundraising? Introduce yourself to the board of a local zoo and volunteer to be on the fundraising committee for an annual event. Look, for example, at nonprofits like the National Zoo in Washington, D.C., which hosts ZooFari, an annual fundraising gala that has, each spring for almost 30 years, brought together 100 of the Washington, D.C., area's finest restaurants and vintners from around the country for an evening of gourmet foods, fine wines, fabulous entertainment, and dancing under the stars. This experience will bring together your skills and expertise, your connections and your knowledge, and your passion in a project squarely in the nonprofit sector.

Skill Marketing

Fascinated by the new venture trends hitting the nonprofit sector? Spending your day job focused on developing market share for consumer goods? Determined to help the homeless learn job and life skills? Find a local nonprofit with a revenue-generating model that pays for such programming to take place. Look, for example, at nonprofits like Haley House in Boston, Massachusetts, whose Bakery Café creates economic sustainability for underemployed women and men and nurtures the local community. Each year through their bakery training program, at least ten underemployed, low-income women and men engage in a six-month training program. While being paid, these trainees—along with their trainers—prepare top-notch food for both the café and wholesale bakery. Once the trainees have successfully completed the program, Haley House helps them get jobs.

Networking

Make sure you also think strategically about whom you want to meet through board service. As in the corporate sector, nonprofits operate on word of mouth, personal connections, and social marketing. Most people who sit on nonprofit boards are also sitting on others or have sat on others in the past. If each nonprofit board averages around eight members, your seven board cohorts can connect you immediately to 56 other nonprofit decision makers.

Finding a Board Seat

The advent of the Internet has brought the board application and nomination process out of the country club and into the mainstream. Many websites exist where board seat seekers can enter their profile and their interests and have board opportunities, both national and local, delivered to their inbox. Nonprofits can post their board needs and seek direct applications or look through a file of résumés for their perfect match.

Web Resources That Match Board Candidates and Nonprofit Boards

Websites:

- BoardnetUSA *(www.BoardnetUSA.org)*

- BoardSource *(www.BoardSource.org)*

- Bridgestar *(www.Bridgestar.org)*

- Volunteer Solutions *(https://volunteer.united-e-way.org/org/board/dir-A-1.html)*

Local nonprofit board fairs:

- National Council of Nonprofit Associations *(www.ncna.org)* lists state chapters that hold board fairs.

- The Council on Foundations *(www.cof.org/Locator/)* hosts a listing of community foundations that will link to your local foundation.

- United Way *(www.unitedway.org)* hosts local fairs through each of its community chapters.

Get Active: Work in the Sector as a Volunteer, Loaned Executive, or Retired Executive

There are many ways to volunteer in the nonprofit sector. You can work for free, for less than full pay, or for full pay by choosing from a variety of options and commitment levels. Independent Sector *(www.IndependentSector.org)* is the leadership forum for charities, foundations, and corporate giving programs committed to advancing the common good in America and around the world. In 2001, it completed a landmark study of the state of volunteerism in America, titled *Giving and Volunteering in the United States.* Based on a national survey of more than 4,000 adults, this series of reports found that 44 percent of the adult population volunteered with a formal organization in 2000, amounting to 83.9 million adults. These adults volunteered approximately 15.5 billion hours of service in 2000 alone, at a value of $239.2 billion. According to Urban Institute, the current value of volunteer time is $20.16 per hour, so consider it real work!

Old-Fashioned Volunteering Made Current

When most of us think of volunteering, we imagine ourselves tutoring children or reading to the elderly. We see our parents leading our childhood scout troops. We remember the sick neighbor to whom we brought nourishing meals. None of that has changed, and all of that is still valuable. Joining a community environmental clean-up project or participating in your neighborhood watch group is important. You should do it, and you should do it often. But let's look at some other, new volunteering options available to you. Instead of spending one Saturday a year cleaning up your local park, get involved in the planning committee that runs clean-up days citywide. Instead of organizing your child's school's monthly bake sale, work with the administration to better track, spend, or invest the proceeds. Instead of spending five hours a month reading to the blind, use that time on a board committee that looks at ways to expand the program to reach more people.

To do this, you first must find an organization that needs what you bring to the table. This shouldn't be hard. As the government continues to cut back assistance and foundations become more selective about what they fund, the needs of nonprofits continue to grow. Set yourself up in a situation where you will be expected to donate at least 100 hours of your time over the course of many months. Most organizations, corporate or nonprofit, have different focuses, workloads, and paces of action depending on the time of year; volunteering deeply will allow you to see the nonprofit sector, and your particular nonprofit of interest, in its many seasons of development, growth, and change.

Second, ensure that you are not just working on the front lines but behind the scenes as well. Again, all volunteering is important, but not all volunteering strategically positions you to get a full-time job in the nonprofit sector. While providing direct service is fulfilling and heartwarming, only an in-depth view of the operations will tell you if this sector is right for you. Further, it will arm you with the right language to tell newly acquired, immediately relevant success stories in your interviews.

Become a Loaned Executive

Loaned executive programs offer corporate transitioners an opportunity to stick a toe in the nonprofit pond before jumping directly into the deep end. These programs allow business professionals to work on discreet projects, at the highest levels in nonprofit administration, for limited amounts of time. Corporations enjoy an enhanced community image, a reduction in internal training costs for high-performing staff, and an increase in the number of staff being groomed for executive leadership positions, while the loaned executive gets trained in fundraising and partnership development, learns up close how a nonprofit operates, and develops deeper insights into community needs and resources.

Web Resources to Help You Get Active

Find a volunteer opportunity:

- 1-800-Volunteer *(www.1-800-volunteer.org)*

- Hands On Network *(www.handsonnetwork.org)*

- Points of Light's Volunteer Centers *(www.pointsoflight.org/centers/find_center.cfm)*

- SERVENet *(www.servenet.org)*

- VolunteerMatch *(www.volunteermatch.org)*

- Volunteer Solutions *(www.volunteersolutions.org)*

Find a loaned executive placement:

- United Way's Loaned Executives *(http://national.unitedway.org)*

- Building Blocks International's Corporate Service Corps *(www.bblocks.org)*

Find a consulting project:

- Executive Service Corps Affiliate Network *(www.escus.org)*

- Taproot Foundation *(www.taprootfoundation.org)*

- Catch-a-fire *(www.catchafire.org)*

Become a Consultant

Another way to make the move into nonprofit work is to become a consultant, either paid or unpaid, as discussed in *Mission Driven*. Becoming a consultant allows you to become involved in important decision-making at critical times in nonprofits you might like to join, as well as giving you valuable insider information about the type of organization, the way it goes about its business, and its approach to change.

Get Smart: Additional Education Comes in Handy

Taking time to earn a nonprofit management degree or attend a leadership program provides a natural segue into the sector. It demonstrates your dedication to move into a nonprofit career while stocking your career kit with the tools you will need to be successful once you've gotten there. Education can be gathered in an undergraduate or graduate university setting, through an executive education or extension course, or by attending one of the many local community leadership programs that exist nationwide.

Corporate Voluntarism[5]

- 81.7 percent of corporations focus their employee volunteer programs on core business functions.

- One out of every two corporations stresses a commitment to community service in its corporate mission statement.

- 58 percent of corporations use their employee volunteer program for recruiting and retaining employees.

Undergraduate and Graduate Degrees

Colleges and universities have responded to the growth of the nonprofit sector with expanded course and degree offerings in the nonprofit area. More than 255 colleges and universities offer degrees in nonprofit management, while others offer stand-alone, noncredit courses. These courses, which may be taught either at the undergraduate or graduate level, have titles like Fundraising, Governance, Strategic Planning, Human Resource Management, and Financial Management. More than a hundred institutions offer a graduate degree in nonprofit management.

A sample listing of these colleges, universities, and training organizations can be found at the end of this book.

Business School

As counterintuitive as it may seem, business school is a perfect way to transition from a corporate career into the nonprofit sector. Business schools understand that a nonprofit's very livelihood rests on its ability to operate effectively and efficiently like its corporate counterparts, and recently, business schools have been attracting more applicants with a nonprofit career as a post-graduation goal. Some schools, like Harvard and Stanford, have even begun offering loan forgiveness programs to their graduates who enter the nonprofit sector after completing their education.

Women are also finding that business schools are using nonprofit degrees as a recruiting tool. Research studies repeatedly show that women more often than men opt for careers that ultimately make a contribution to society. Studies also show that they make graduate school choices, like medicine or law, that allow them to start their education immediately upon college graduation so that they can start a career before a family. New thinking in business schools, such as adjusting the required years of work experience for admission, has allowed women to pursue their MBA earlier, giving them the luxury of doing what was not an option for their mothers and grandmothers: flexibility while fulfilling their own personal and professional goals.

A list of the top nonprofit MBA programs can be found at the back of this book.

---

5. *The Corporate Volunteer Program as a Strategic Resource: The Link Grows Stronger* (Washington, D.C.: Points of Light Foundation, 2000).

Executive Education

MBA programs are more and more often offering midcareer programs with specializations in nonprofit management. Harvard, Stanford, and Georgetown lead the list of highly ranked, competitive programs that have begun offering courses with names like the following:

- Governing for Nonprofit Excellence
- Performance Measurement for Effective Management of Nonprofit Organizations
- Public Leadership: Principles, Practices, and Realities
- Public Policy, Advocacy, and Social Change
- Strategic Perspectives in Nonprofit Management
- Philanthropy and Public Policy
- Strategy for Nonprofit Organizations

Most of these programs are offered in the evenings or on weekends, catering to a working professional's busy schedule. Participating in one of these programs offers deep and current knowledge, a ready-made network, and access to the university's graduate and continuing professional education career office.

Leadership Programs

Many nonprofit organizations exist locally, statewide, or even regionally to bring together nonprofit and corporate leaders around issues of pressing need. Through a carefully run application and acceptance process, they compile a diverse and dynamic annual "class" that comes together throughout a given year to discuss, learn, and cooperate around solutions to challenges. These programs make for exceptional educational and networking opportunities as well as lending a "seal of approval" to your résumé.

Nonprofit Management Certificates and Specializations

More than 50 graduate schools nationwide offer nonprofit certificate programs for those without the time, energy, or resources to commit to an advanced degree in a university setting. Most of the certificates are in nonprofit management or leadership, with the balance covering specific areas like arts administration, fundraising, association management, and the like. Coursework in these programs is similar to topics covered more rigorously in graduate programs, and it often focuses specifically on best practices without delving deeply into the research and theory behind them.

An illustrative listing of all of these educational programs can be found at the back of this book.

Conclusion

Writing a résumé often feels like cleaning out the attic. It seems like a good idea at first, but then halfway through, you begin to wonder why you ever started. Rest assured that the time and effort you put into writing and rewriting this vital marketing piece will make you a better networker and, ultimately, interviewee. In fact, it's likely to make you a better nonprofit employee as well.

The résumé is only part of your marketing package. You also need to worry about your cover letter, your interviewing style, and your references. Let's move on to those now.

Testimonials from Successful Career Changers:

Cherry Muse, *Executive Director,*
Public Conversations Project, Watertown, Massachusetts

An attorney by training, Cherry was sworn in as a member of the Massachusetts Bar on the due date for her first child. Over the next five years, she and her husband had two other children, all the while balancing her role as an attorney with her role as a mother. She worked part-time, practicing law and developing a mediation practice. As her children started school, she became an active volunteer and, because of her legal background, was asked to serve on a number of committees and task forces that had a substantive impact on her town. "I found that I liked being a change agent," she says, "and discovered that most often, I quickly became a leader wherever I served. This was a surprise, as I had never seen myself that way before." When her youngest child approached middle school age, Cherry decided to enter the nonprofit sector full-time.

Cherry's first job in the nonprofit sector was as associate program director for the Anti-Defamation League, a position that pulled together many of her volunteer activities—building community, supporting human rights, strengthening education, and supporting the Jewish community. Eighteen months later, she became associate director of development. Cherry has also worked as director of development for YouthBuild USA and executive director of The Wellness Community—Greater Boston before becoming executive director of the Public Conversations Project. A good deal of her experience has been in founder-driven organizations.

How did the culture of the nonprofit sector comport with Cherry's work-life balance?

As a volunteer, Cherry had the luxury of picking and choosing her projects and activities. "I could set limits," she explains, "but that became considerably more difficult when I was a staff member." Cherry found that the nonprofit sector's self-selected population of mission-driven employees, especially her two founder-visionary bosses, made it difficult at first for her to establish boundaries and maintain a healthy work-life balance. "There have been times I felt myself getting competitive about who could work more and would find myself waking up earlier and earlier to get to the office first!"

she remembers. "Fortunately, when my inner workaholic tried to emerge, my family helped me to set limits on myself."

What steps did Cherry take when she determined that she would find her next career in the nonprofit sector?

Cherry began collecting appealing newspaper help-wanted ads, even if she wasn't remotely qualified for the position. "After doing this for several months," she explains, "I went back and re-read the ads to see what they told me about myself." When an ad appeared for a nonprofit whose mission she knew she could embrace, she jumped. Since then, Cherry's three subsequent nonprofit jobs have come through a combination of networking and responding to ads—this time on the Internet instead of the newspaper.

How did Cherry grow from a practicing mediation attorney into a nonprofit executive director?

Shortly after being hired for her first nonprofit job, it became clear to Cherry that to develop professionally, she would need fundraising experience. "I sought to become associate development director," she explains, "and my successive career moves were all possible because I added the fundraising component early on in my career." In addition, Cherry credits as part of her success the fact that she entered the nonprofit sector with career and volunteer experience behind her. Having served on multiple boards made her less intimidated by board members. "I had a clearer sense of what board members and volunteers wanted, because I had been a board member and volunteer myself."

Cherry's Key Lessons Learned:

- ✓ "Being in the nonprofit field is no excuse for sloppiness, either in the workplace or in an interview. The same high standards for professionalism apply."
- ✓ "Volunteering is an excellent way to get a sense of whether this is a world you'd like to enter."
- ✓ "Get some fundraising experience, as a board member or just as a volunteer. The nonprofit will love you, you'll do some good in the world, and you'll be adding some valuable experience to your résumé."

Aude Thibaut, *Major Donor Development Manager*, The Royal Opera House, Covent Garden, London, England

One year after landing one of the most coveted finance jobs in her whole graduating MBA class, Aude realized that she was spending the majority of her waking hours doing things that didn't inspire her. While her career was mentally stimulating, it failed to move her soul. "It became apparent that my primary passion outside work was classical vocal music," she explains, "so I decided that I should try and find a job that would use my corporate skills not to make money but to make a difference and enjoy my day-to-day." What began as a simple line of questioning became a career in fundraising for the Royal Opera House in London.

Moving from banking into the arts provided quite a challenge for Aude. Because her previous experience seemed so unrelated to what she saw as her future career, applying for jobs through typical channels would lead only to her resume being dismissed on sight. "Naively, I was surprised that human resources officers at arts organizations didn't read 'Goldman Sachs' and on my resume and think, 'Wow, we must have her!'" With pedigrees from the Sorbonne, the London School of Economics, and Columbia Business School, Aude had an interesting dilemma on her hands.

What steps did Aude take to find her nonprofit job?

Aude had to translate her experience in banking into terms that could be understood by arts organizations. With the help of a specialized arts headhunter who helped her go over her resume line by line, Aude repackaged herself for the search. "Quickly, it became apparent that the best fit for me would be in fundraising," she explains, "and so I did a voluntary, unpaid, three-month internship with an opera company in their fundraising department to show that I was committed to the mission and knew what I was getting myself into."

Aude found her position exclusively through networking with her contacts. "Fortunately," she found, "in the nonprofit sector, people are ready to meet with you very easily if you ask them for advice. One introduction—from a banker friend who had met a woman running a music festival on a plane to Boston—led to another, and I found myself in front of the development director of the opera company, who gave me an internship."

Will Aude's next position be in the nonprofit sector?

No. Aude feels that she has found the organization that she believes in. She enjoys what she does and feels compelled by the mission of the organization. For her, moving into the nonprofit sector was about following a specific passion rather than an overall sense of doing good. "If you go in with a purpose and a passion, you won't mind for a second any of the inefficiencies or necessary drudge work that comes even to the most qualified managers. I believe in the Royal Opera House and I wouldn't work for another nonprofit just because it is a nonprofit."

Aude's Key Lessons Learned:

✓ "Meet as many people as you can. Jump at any contact that is thrown at you. Meet them, get more contacts from them, and talk to more people. You will find that people are always ready to give their time to impart advice."

✓ "Use your networking time preciously. All the people you meet during your search will remain valuable contacts after it, but because you will be affiliated with an institution by then, your access and relationship may change."

✓ "Don't just 'work in nonprofit.' If you're passionate about the environment, then focus on it. If you are indignant about domestic abuse or the treatment of women, work for an organization that helps them. Don't go into the nonprofit sector like people go into the corporate sector, just because of some vague idea that draws you there. Follow your passion."

CHAPTER 3:

Cover Letters, Interviews, and References

While the résumé gets you noticed, cover letters, interviews, and references get you the job. They are part of the overall package you present and should be treated with as much importance as your résumé. In fact, these supporting materials, actions, and testimonials likely will set you apart from the other applicants in the pool, getting you greater consideration at decision-making time.

As a job seeker coming from the corporate sector, your cover letters, interviews, and references are your opportunity to show that you not only know the nonprofit sector and have a track record of dedication or success in a certain mission area, but have thought strategically and deeply about what this transition will be like for you and the organization you ultimately serve. This chapter will walk you through how to write cover letters that resonate in the nonprofit sector, how to approach and master the nonprofit interview, and how to use your corporate and nonprofit references strategically to get that dream job.

The Importance of Cover Letters

As mentioned in Chapter 2, the biggest secret in headhunting is that recruiters read cover letters last. The word *cover* shouldn't even be included in *cover letter*, because most headhunters staple it to the back of a résumé once opened. In fact, by the time most headhunters look at your cover letter, they feel you are at least somewhat qualified and want to know more.

Before you stop reading this chapter, remember that any materials that make it as far as a "hold" pile will be read, from cover letters to references to anything extra, like addendums of publications or presentations. It is then that cover letters matter most—and even more so for sector switchers—as they distinguish intriguing possibilities from average, everyday candidates. A cover letter adds another dimension to your application. It shows the recruiter that you can write and, most importantly for career changers, it answers the obvious questions: Why the nonprofit sector? Why this nonprofit in particular? And why now?

However, cover letters can also be quicksand for candidates. From easy-to-catch mistakes like forgetting to change the name of the company in the address block or misspelling the hiring manager's name, to larger issues of quantity, substance, and tone, a bad cover letter can torpedo your hopes of landing an interview and, ultimately, your nonprofit job.

Four-Paragraph Cover Letter Outline

Cover letters should be one page and run about three to four paragraphs, comprising your introduction, relevant passion, skills and qualifications, and any specific information about your current situation and contact information. Note that missing from this list—as they waste valuable space, may be illegal, and are certainly irrelevant, as discussed in Chapter 2—are references to age, height, weight, marital status, number and age of children, hobbies, race, religion, pets, or the results of your last physical. Just like with your résumé, do not, under any circumstances, ever attach your picture to the cover letter, unless you are responding to a call from the Barbizon School of Modeling, and even then, proceed with caution.

The following is a simple, four-paragraph outline that you can follow to take the guesswork out of writing your cover letter. Your first cover letter will be the hardest. After that, you will find that you can cut and paste a good deal to make the process more efficient.

Paragraph #1: An Introduction

Everyone reads the first paragraph of any letter they receive. Agonizing over this paragraph will further improve the "elevator speech" that you began developing in Chapter 1 of *Mission Driven*, because this is where you tell the reader what you are applying for and why, ever so briefly, you think you are the right candidate for the position. If you can't come up with something to say in this paragraph, take some time to consider if this is the right job for you. Perhaps you should be looking at jobs in organizations with missions closer to your heart or with different levels of seniority, responsibility, or expertise.

Make sure you are specific about the job in question, because most managers are hiring for more than one job at a time. Also, make sure to specify how you heard about the job. If you heard about it from an individual known to the staff, a recruiter, a hiring manager, or a job board, be sure to drop that name.

If you read about a position as an advertisement on a website or in a print publication, write that in your cover letter. After all, advertising costs money, and most nonprofits lack both a human resources department and a human resources budget. Being strapped for cash, they'll want to know which advertising brought them interesting candidates like you. In the interview, you'll get asked where you heard about this position, and if you can't remember or, worse, say that you "are applying for lots of jobs and must have seen it on one of the many websites," you simply won't sound smart—nor will the interviewer feel special. This is, after all, a wooing process. Better to hedge your bets and list it right up front in the cover letter.

A note on little white lies: if you get caught off guard when you get asked where you saw the job announcement and can't remember—probably because you did, in fact, see it on one of the many job websites you've researched—you can tell a teeny fib here and get away with it. The best answer in this situation is that you don't know where it was originally posted, but that it was referred to you by a colleague who knows your work as well as your desire to work for this particular mission area and thought it would be a perfect match for your skills, expertise, and passion. Someone who knows your work and thinks that you would be right for this job is about as close to a pre-interview reference as you can get. In this situation, your answer sends the message that you have already passed a hurdle in a professional setting and raises your candidacy to the same level as that of other nonprofit candidates who have proven themselves in more familiar settings.

Goal for Paragraph #1:
This may be the only paragraph of your letter that is read. The aim of this paragraph is to tell the reader quickly for which position you wish to be considered and where you saw it advertised and to give them a quick sell.

Sample Paragraph #1:
Please find attached my résumé in application for the position of _____ as posted on _____. My combination of _____ and _____, combined with my passion for _____, makes me an ideal candidate for this position.

Paragraph #2: A Little about Them

What is everyone's favorite subject of conversation? Themselves, of course. After you've told the reader what you are applying for and why, briefly, you would be the ideal candidate, tell a bit about what you know about the organization and its current needs. These paragraphs often start off something like, "The Nature Conservancy has long been a leader in . . ." or, "As times have changed, National Geographic has been able to . . ." and continue on to, "From reading your website, I was excited to learn about the new direction you are taking . . ."

Doing a little homework will separate you from the rest of the candidates. Of course, your reader already knows about the current challenges facing the organization, but the hirer doesn't know that *you* know—and doesn't know that you know it in the language of the nonprofit sector. The "Insert Job Here" cover letter won't work under normal circumstances, and it especially doesn't work for sector switchers. Talk about the organization's current work and segue back to how it blends with your career. This leads nicely into paragraph three, where you tell a little about how your skills dovetail with the organization's needs.

Goal for Paragraph #2:

Tell them a little about themselves to show that you've done some homework and understand where they are as an organization and where they want to be. Alternative phrases you can use in this paragraph include: "In my conversations with . . .", "From your website, I learned . . .", or, "In my work with . . ."

Sample Paragraph #2:

The Good Foundation has long been a leader in _____, and I read with great excitement about the new direction your technology department is taking. I would greatly enjoy becoming a member of the team that will bring a better use of technology to your grantees. My experience to date has been in the area of digital divide issues as they affect organizations that . . . .

Paragraph #3: A Little about You

Now that you've told the hiring manager what you know about the organization and its current challenges, communicate what, specifically, you have done that qualifies you to get them to where they need to be. Pull from your paid and unpaid work your achievements skills that make you certain that you can be successful in this role. If the only relevant experience you've had has been as a volunteer, then lean heavily on this, but don't ignore that you've had paid work experience as well.

Don't feel you need to outline your entire professional history, as some of it will be irrelevant and most of it will be repetitive. Again, by the time the hiring manager has gotten to your cover letter, your résumé has already conveyed that you are at least in some way qualified. Now the hirer is trying to understand better why you are interested in this move at this time. Write up your professional history to read more like a strategic argument about why you should be interviewed rather than a rote recitation of your résumé.

Paragraph #3:

And so on, specifically about how your skills and experience will help the organization meet the challenge at hand. By this time, your interviewer has seen your résumé and feels your experience at least merits further investigation. The hiring manager now wants to know why you are interested in this job. This will be the longest paragraph of your one-page cover letter, comprising four or five sentences, and should answer the following questions: Why are you right for this position? What skills do you bring that are relevant to the challenges we face?

Sample Paragraph #3:

Specifically, as one of the first participants in the United Way's Corporate Technology Partners Program, I enabled _____ organization to _____. Prior to that, I . . . .

Paragraph #4: Contact Information and Current Situation

Once you've made your quick pitch, shown your smarts, and tied your background to the organization's needs, all that's left is to tell the reader how to contact you. You are a great candidate, after all, and they need to know this information. Nonprofits don't generally have lots of extra printers and faxes sitting around, so cover letters and second pages of résumés often find their way into other people's stacks of paper. If your cover letter looks great but your résumé didn't follow, or vice versa, some contact information in the letter will come in quite handy.

If you are currently leaving your job for a reason worth sharing with the hiring manager—perhaps a sickness in the family has meant that you can't travel as often as your job demands, but because of which you are now interested in helping your prospective future employer cure this disease—this is the place to list it. Folks in the nonprofit sector will assume that you are making this change because of some form of enlightenment, and being up front about it will increase your chances of seeming real. Lists of corporate sector jobs aren't necessarily that interesting, but coupling them with a human touch is.

Goal for Paragraph #4:

Don't say that you look forward to learning more about the job or the organization; that's not your prospective employer's burden. Remember to create a letterhead with all of your contact information, including e-mail address. Be sure to note if you are in a cubicle or have a public voice mail, or you risk letting your boss know about your job search before you are ready.

Sample Paragraph #4:

I look forward to speaking to you soon about my qualifications and experiences. I can be reached at _____ during the day or _____ in the evenings.

Make It Real to Them

One of the biggest frustrations that nonprofit hiring managers have with corporate applicants is language that seems to go in circles, or corporate-speak that doesn't seem ever to come down to telling what you actually accomplished at the end of the day. A nonprofit hiring manager will be impatient with any job seeker introducing themselves this way but especially with a someone looking to transition out of corporate life. Already they may have a prejudice against sector switchers, having seen too many who believe, "Nonprofits would be better off if they were run like corporations." Starting off the cover letter in corporate-speak, or by telling them how wonderful you and your corporate work have been, will only serve to deepen those prejudices.

Give your recruiter something relevant and substantial to chew on in the cover letter. Choose three or four key responsibilities from the position description and explain clearly and concisely where you have successfully managed projects or tasks of comparable size and complexity in your career. Be sure to tie your experience back to past or probable future success in the nonprofit arena. Here are some examples.

Prejudice Deepener #1: While I was at The Great Corporation, we incorporated CQI into our new product rollout.

Prejudice Reliever #1: Just as you are trying to do as you expand your program into five new cities, while at The Great Corporation, I spearheaded work to ensure that the quality of our product remained high while we entered new markets and sought out new customers.

Prejudice Deepener #2: In my last start-up, I raised $50 million in venture capital seed funding.

Prejudice Reliever #2: While most of my fundraising experience has been with venture capitalists, such as raising $50 million in seed funding for my last start-up, I believe that the skills I acquired to research prospects, develop relationships, and steward funders will translate well to the capital campaign on which you are about to embark.

Showing Your True Colors

Whether you have experience in a specific nonprofit field or are looking to shift into a new arena, explaining your passion in your cover letter can provide much-needed depth to your paper presentation. To paraphrase John F. Kennedy, "Ask not what your employer can do for you, but what you can do for your employer." The same is true for cover letters.

For example, no employer will get excited over the possibility of providing a "challenging and fulfilling opportunity where a generous salary can be earned while serving others." Most employers, on the other hand, will race to the phone to call a candidate that is "inspired by the opportunity to ensure adequate health care for underprivileged children while contributing to the long-term financial sustainability of the parent organization."

Nonprofits are excited about your interest in their universe. They are happy whenever anyone has realized that their issue area is critical and demands the dedication of anyone's full attention.

Go bold! Tell them about your experiences as a child, as a mother, as a friend. Reveal your true colors, not as a corporate hack but as a warm-blooded, idealistic, passionate individual worth getting to know.

Applying via E-Mail

The best and fastest way to apply, if given the opportunity, is via e-mail. It is the most direct method of communication and the least likely to get lost in a pile of papers on an overburdened hiring manager's desk. It makes it easy for a hiring manager to review your application while on the road, forward your résumé to superiors, and expedite the hiring process.

In this day and age of Internet viruses, the worst thing you can do is send a blank e-mail with your cover letter and résumé as attachments. Simply putting the words "See Attached" won't work either. Would you open an e-mail or its attachments from a total stranger? Given that hiring managers get attachments all day long and are extra vigilant about viruses, they'll likely not open yours, or they may just put off opening them until they are distracted by another candidate and have forgotten all about you.

Instead, attach your résumé to the e-mail and insert the body of your cover letter in the text of the e-mail. Attaching your résumé preserves the formatting and style of your document, while inserting the cover letter allows you to make your pitch before the hiring manager makes a hasty judgment about a résumé filled with corporate work. It's highly possible that in the application instructions, you were asked to follow directions about the subject line of your e-mail, perhaps to insert the job title or your name; always follow those directions.

Top Ten Cover Letter Dos and Don'ts

1. **Do** keep it to one page.

2. **Don't** be so brief that the employer must go on safari to find information.

3. **Do** personalize each letter, making the case about this mission and this nonprofit.

4. **Don't** misspell the name of the human resources manager, headhunter, or organization.

5. **Do** craft each cover letter to the specific job and recruiter, mentioning the position and organization in the first sentence.

6. **Don't** load the letter with corporate jargon, acronyms, or the latest business guru's ideas.

7. **Do** match your skills, whether gained in paid work or through volunteerism, to the job responsibilities.

8. **Don't** include charts and tables.

9. **Do** set yourself out as unique among a potential applicant pool because of your track record and passion.

10. **Don't** distinguish yourself with paper so unique it detracts from the content of the cover letter and résumé.

Three Sample Cover Letters:

Cover Letter Strategy #1: Wearing Your Heart on Your Sleeve

Jennifer Jobseeker
149 Main Street
Tallahassee, Florida
jennifer_jobseeker@email.com (904) 555-8594

April 17, 2014

Janice Searchchair
Search Committee Chair
415 Broadway
Somerville, Massachusetts 02144

Dear Ms. Searchchair,

I read with great interest the recent recruitment announcement for the position of executive director of the National Infertility Support Center on the Nonprofit Professionals Advisory Group website and would welcome the opportunity to explore it further.

Six million people in the United States suffer from infertility; I am one of them. I joined the National Infertility Support Center over ten years ago and found support and education through its exceptional services. I have often found myself telling both men and women to contact the National Infertility Support Center so that they, too, will not be alone while dealing with the difficult mental, emotional, and financial issues brought about because of infertility. More can be done, and through the National Infertility Support Center's comprehensive national network of chapters, the organization is extremely well positioned to transform the public's awareness of infertility and develop the financial resources to bring about change.

For the last 15 years, I have devoted myself to leading, managing, and increasing the influence of nonprofit organizations. Performing this function for the National Infertility Support Center, a highly respected national organization in whose mission I strongly believe, would be both challenging and exciting to me. It would be a culmination of my personal experience with and passion for infertility support and solutions, organizational leadership experience, and political expertise. I have spent my career in the nexus of public policy, advocacy, and change, all powered by the action and involvement of individuals wanting to make a difference. The passion behind the National Infertility Support Center is no different.

The specific qualifications noted in the job description correspond directly with my experience and the leadership roles that I have held, both as an executive director and a consultant to nonprofit organizations. These positions required extensive government and political acumen; the development and implementation of lobbying strategies on both a statewide and national level; direct support of highly engaged board members and volunteers; coalition building; fundraising through memberships, grants, and grassroots fundraising; the development of innovative programs; collaborations with a wide range of constituencies; and financial and staff management.

My expertise and abilities, coupled with my personal experience, make me an ideal candidate for this position. It would be my honor to assist the National Infertility Support Center in raising its voice, honing its programs and messages, and reaching its ultimate potential.

Thank you for your consideration.

Sincerely,
Jennifer JobSeeker

Cover Letter Strategy #2: Selling Your Corporate Experience to a Nonprofit

Eugene JobSeeker
1304 Main Street
Cincinnati, Ohio 45205
bruce.jobseeker@email.com (513) 555-0885

April 21, 2014

Paul Headhunter
Williams Search Associates
6937 Main Street
Philadelphia, Pennsylvania 19131

Dear Mr. Headhunter,

Please find attached my résumé in response to your recent announcement for a finance director for the Young Charitable Foundation. My proven track record managing financial, administrative, human resources, legal, and tax matters for a company of similar size and complexity, combined with my deeply held desire to improve the capacity of our neighborhood youth service organizations, makes me an ideal candidate for this position.

Inner-city neighborhoods across the country are just turning the corner. The work of the Young Charitable Foundation to reward organizations doing good work with the opportunity to do more and better work has caught on, and foundations across the country are striving to emulate your success, while your benefactors are asking you to replicate and grow. It is a difficult but exciting place to be. As you navigate your expected growth trajectory, my experience may provide a valuable road map of success.

Since January of 1999, I have served as the director of administration and finance for the Northside Corporation. In this role, I designed and implemented all systems and infrastructure necessary for the efficient and smooth running of the organization. The organization experienced rapid and sizable growth soon after my tenure began, its asset base quadrupling and its needs for enhanced systems, space, and structures increasing. I have overseen or performed all duties required to turn a small group of staff members into a well-respected and well-oiled company, from setting up office space, hiring staff, and instituting and managing annual audits to searching for and interviewing more investment managers, investment advisors, attorneys, and various other consultants, as well as creating and implementing more complicated internal controls and policies. In addition, I have had the honor of working with the corporation's board, formalizing agendas and minutes, ensuring compliance with bylaws, and acquiring directors' and officers' insurance.

I am interested in joining the nonprofit sector full-time in a role that is both professionally demanding and personally fulfilling. My passion remains with neighborhood investment, and my skill set would be ideal for a foundation that is in the midst of early growth and change. My track record overseeing finance and investments throughout the past 25 years would allow me to contribute substantially. I look forward to speaking with you soon.

Thank you for your consideration.

Sincerely,
Eugene JobSeeker

Cover Letter Strategy #3:
Bringing Your Nonprofit Volunteer Work Front and Center

Barbara JobSeeker
655 Norbury Drive
Austin, Texas
barjobseek@email.com (512) 555-9144

February 12, 2014

Kathryn HiringManager, PhD
Executive Director
Earth Friendly USA
Washington, DC
Via E-mail: khm@email.org

Dear Dr. HiringManager:

Mary Johnson recently told me about your search for a chief operating officer for Earth Friendly USA. My financial and administrative acumen and strategic management experience, combined with my experience working with mission-driven nonprofit organizations, make me an ideal candidate for this position.

I am particularly interested in your strategic use of volunteer opportunities and education to catalyze change. I served as a board member for Greener Group Texas, an organization that managed more than 2,300 volunteers annually and built its success on harnessing the power of volunteers to become effective advocates. We built our volunteer programs with the express purpose of developing a strong, educated response to rising oil prices as well as providing service and meaningful volunteer experiences. Our success in mobilizing volunteers and changing minds was inspiring and changed the course of fuel usage in this state. I witnessed, firsthand, how efficient and intelligent internal management can enable an organization to focus on building more effective programs and advocacy. I have spent my career at the crossroads where innovative management meets the creation of change, and I believe my skills and experience may be a good fit for Earth Friendly USA.

Specifically, as chair of the finance committee, I was responsible for the management of Greener Group Texas's financial and administrative operations and helped transform it from a small grassroots nonprofit with a budget of $4 million into a nationally recognized leader in the field of environmental advocacy with a budget of $11 million and a reserve in excess of $3 million. As we grew, I oversaw all day-to-day organizational management and short- and long-term business and strategic planning before we had a permanent staff in place. Eventually, I led the newly formed senior management team for finance, administration, human resources, development, programs, and advocacy.

At this point in my career, I am looking to work with a nonprofit advocacy organization where my management experience, ability to deliver strong operating results, sense of humor, and passion for mission can be of use. I can be reached at barjobseek@email.com or (512) 555-9144 to schedule a convenient time to meet and discuss my qualifications and interest in this position. Thank you for considering my application.

Sincerely,
Barbara JobSeeker

Answering the Salary Question

Application instructions often ask for salary history or salary expectations. This is one of the hardest directives to which a sector switcher must respond. Comparing your corporate salary compensation package to your nonprofit compensation package is like comparing apples to oranges. Actually, it's more like comparing apples to hubcaps. The sectors' pay ranges have little in common, and the valuation of jobs is completely different. There are still, however, great opportunities to earn a living wage while getting more fulfillment, a nicer lifestyle, and more opportunities to lead change in return.

Many job announcements ask for you to respond with a résumé, cover letter, and salary history. Nonprofits do this because they don't know what they need to pay to get the right person in the job. Most haven't done a salary survey in years, if not decades, and many aren't aware of current market rates.

If you aren't asked in the cover letter, this question might come up at any stage of the job search cycle, and more often than not catches candidates—especially career changers—off guard. You may be asked up front, as you start an informational call, or the subject might not arise until you get to the offer stage. It could be slipped in anywhere, so you need to be prepared to deal with it. Mishandling this question will likely sound the death knell of your negotiating power or will certainly show your ignorance of the nonprofit sector. Let's look at several strategies to help deal with the salary question.

Avoiding the Question: Taking the Fifth

One option is to ignore the question, but you choose this option at your own risk. Remember, headhunters ask for this information because its something they need to know. Not telling them makes you look as though you are either avoiding the question, not following directions, or feel that the rules don't apply to you. Given that you are switching sectors, your knowledge and acceptance of the fact that nonprofits pay on a different scale, as discussed in *Mission Driven*, is key to getting an interview.

If you feel you must avoid the question, you ought at least to acknowledge that it was asked. At least this way, the headhunter knows you understand its importance but are choosing to put it off to another date. Say something like, "My salary history from the corporate sector would make little sense in this context, as my skills and expertise were judged by an entirely different set of goals. This move into the nonprofit sector is not motivated by financial needs, although I would expect to be paid according to the level of skills and experiences sought in the position."

Polite Ways of Skirting a Salary Question When First Asked
- "I'd be happy to talk about that at the appropriate time. Why don't you tell me more about the job?"
- "Before we get to that, let me make sure I'm even in your ballpark. What is the salary range for this position?"
- "I'm not comfortable discussing salary at this stage. Perhaps we can do so when we meet in person?"
- "My current employer does not allow me to discuss the terms of my employment."
- "For the skills and experience you want, I'd expect that this position would not pay less than $_____. Correct?"

Be Prepared for These Pushy Responses
- "We don't have a salary range but would like to learn more about the market. What are you making now?"
- "I need to know because my boss/client will ask, and they won't consider anyone without a complete file."
- "I'm afraid I cannot consider your application without your complete history."
- "I understand that you may have taken a salary cut for this position, so give me your last few salaries as well."
- "I'd hate to waste your time. Let's make sure we can afford you before we get too far down the road."

Know When to Say When

The compensation negotiation is often seen as the last battle of a war, when in fact it is the homecoming dance of the courtship. For the relationship to lead to a happy marriage, neither side should leave the table with their pride hurt or their feelings damaged. It is fine to push back when questioned about your current compensation, but know when to give in. If you don't, you risk coming off as entitled or unable to transition into the nonprofit sector. Remember, the employer has yet to pop the question, and there are still plenty more fish in the sea.

When you feel the time is right is disclose this information—and it's usually fairly obvious—remember that compensation includes more than just salary. A paycheck of $75,000 with benefits equaling $25,000 means that your next employer will need to compensate you in excess of $100,000 to make up the difference in benefits. That being said, the nonprofit sector can offer intangible but nonetheless valuable "compensation," such as title inflation, more flexible work hours, additional opportunity, and the chance to make a living doing something you really love. After all, being stressed out about the planning of logistics for an upcoming conference that will train youth workers to assist the homeless is a lot different than losing sleep over the same logistics for a conference telling a bunch of shareholders how much money the company made for them this quarter.

You Cannot Tell a Lie

At some point during the salary discussion, you may be tempted to enhance, exaggerate, expand, or just plain lie. Don't do it. Headhunters and human resources professionals are a crafty lot, and if they catch you in your lie (and they always will), you will lose credibility, lose the job opportunity, and probably lose every chance to be considered for any jobs with which they may be associated.

Remember that you can always tell them the context around which your salary was determined and what you know to be the true market value of your skills and experience.

Getting More Information about Salary Ranges in the Nonprofit Sector

Many factors affect what a nonprofit can and will pay, including the level of supervisory/managerial responsibility, the type of organization, the number of employees, the annual budget, the scope of the organization, and its geographic area. There are three ways to determine whether your financial needs are in the ballpark of the job for which you are applying.

First, you can look up the most recent tax return—Form 990—of the nonprofit at GuideStar (*www.guidestar.org*). The salaries of the top five highest-paid employees and the outlays to the top five highest-paid consultants are listed on this tax return. If you are not applying for one of the top positions, you can still see the overall salary budget line to get a sense of the overall ranges from this information.

Second, you can get a more general sense of your likely salary by looking up the tax returns of the competitors of the organization, or of other local organizations with similar budgets, missions, and staff sizes. Looking up a three-person hospital foundation won't tell you anything about what the three-person American Heart Association of Providence will pay, but looking up the local American Cancer Society of neighboring Boston might.

Third, you can do some general homework about nonprofit salary averages across the country by reading the many annual salary surveys available. Two of the best include:

1. The *Nonprofit Times* (*www.nptimes.com*). Publishes a free annual salary survey every February.

2. *Abbott, Langer, and Associates* (*www.abbott-langer.com*). Can run up to $375 but is exceptionally comprehensive. It surveys more than a hundred benchmark jobs and describes the highest-paid job characteristics, the national median total cash compensation, and the factors affecting salary rates.

Mastering the Nonprofit Interview

Many job seekers coming from the corporate sector come to the interview process thinking that they will do the nonprofit world a favor by bringing their corporate expertise into the social sector. As we discussed in Chapter 4 of *Mission Driven*, the interviewer on the other side of the table likely doesn't see it that way. You've heard the old expression: you never get a second chance to make a first impression. But what you haven't heard is that most interviewers will size you up within the first ten minutes of an interview. If you don't make a good impression immediately, or if you come across as interested only in putting your corporate stamp on their social mission, you risk spending the balance of your interview with a person who is smiling politely but mentally reviewing their grocery list.

Beat out "milk, cereal, eggs, bread . . ." by meticulously preparing for each phase of the interview. Wow them at the handshake and keep them engaged until, "This way to your new office."

Remember, if you are being asked in for an interview, they have already decided that you are at least remotely interesting in some way. They wouldn't spend their time with you otherwise. All that is left for you to do is wow them with more of your hard work, preparation, and dedication to making a difference to the constituency they serve.

Phase One: Mind Your Appearance

Unlike many things in life, looking your best at an interview is entirely within your control. You know it's coming, you have time to prepare, and you can take full advantage of that. You'll likely look better than you do on a typical work day, and the interviewer knows it. Wear clean, pressed clothes, but keep in mind the type of nonprofit with which you are interviewing. The navy blue, pinstriped suit will work with a foundation in New York City but might not mesh with a grassroots advocacy agency in Albuquerque, New Mexico.

On interview day, bring extra copies of your résumé, business cards, a pad, and pens. You never know when a one-on-one interview will turn into a series of interviews. Don't wear excessive jewelry, makeup, or cologne; this isn't a date. Remember that nonprofits will accept and even nurture your funkier side, but try not to be too funky, or you might distract your interviewers from the words coming out of your mouth. You can wear your horn-rimmed glasses, but leave your alligator skin attaché case at home.

Dealing with a More Sensitive Crowd

Get there early, or have the courtesy to call if you are running late. At best, an interviewer may be able to move other appointments to accommodate you. At worst, the interviewer will seethe through whatever time is left in the scheduled interview. A firm—and, please, dry—handshake is always appreciated. Don't bring stale smoke or (does it need to be said?) alcohol breath into an interview.

Keep your body language in mind. You don't want to come across as "too corporate" by sitting in a closed, tight, defensive position. Be sure to display enthusiasm and warmth, as well as an openness to what your nonprofit interviewer may see as your potential challenges in this career change. Upon seeing that you are open to required change, the interviewer will be more open to giving you a chance. When in doubt, mirror your interviewer, a seasoned nonprofit professional, and you'll come off as the same.

Examples of Positive and Negative Body Language

Positive Body Language:

Openness and warmth:

- Smiling showing teeth
- Open hands with palms visible
- Open coat when seated
- Eye contact without intense staring
- Legs crossed at ankles, not knees
- Deep belly breathing
- Good posture standing and sitting

Confidence:

- Leaning forward in chair
- Chin up
- Interlaced fingers
- Hands joined behind back when standing
- Dry, firm handshake
- Maintaining one to two positions
- Articulation without much gesticulation

Negative Body Language:

Nervousness:

- Whistling
- Fidgeting, constant shifting of position
- Jiggling pocket contents
- Running tongue along front of teeth
- Repeated clearing of throat
- Rubbing back of neck or running fingers through hair
- Wringing hands
- Tongue clicking or a dry mouth

Untrustworthiness or defensiveness:

- Frown or tight grin
- Squinting eyes
- Arms crossed in front of chest
- Pulling away
- Chin down
- Touching nose or face
- Darting eyes before or during answers
- Gestures with fists, chopping hands, or pointing fingers
- Clasping hands behind head while leaning back in the chair

Another important tip: Be friendly to the voice on the other end of the phone when making an appointment. Candidates who abuse administrative staff get ratted out. They don't get second interviews, no matter how qualified they are. Remember, this is the nonprofit sector, where every voice counts and every vote is heard, from the executive director to the intern of three weeks. A receptionist is as likely to sink you as the vice president for development.

Phase Two: Above All, Know Thyself, the Organization, and Its Needs

What has your past work experience done for your ability to help this organization get to where it wants to be? If you don't already know this, slowly step away from the interviewer's office and put your hands up. You aren't ready.

Think through how you wish to portray each job you have held, both the out-of-the-park successes and the sink-to-the-basement disasters. Rehearse your transitions between jobs. You will be asked about all of this, and while you shouldn't grumble about a previous employer, fudging through an obviously tough situation will make you look dishonest. Following are some examples of how to handle questions about past employment:

- **Backwards-looking grumble.** My old boss wasn't too flexible about my personal needs. He just couldn't understand what was happening with my family, so I had to quit.

- **Forward-facing action step**. When my mother fell ill with cancer, I realized that my old position wouldn't allow me the flexibility I needed to take care of her at such an important time, so my boss and I agreed to part ways. Now that my mother has recovered, I have had time to reflect on my own priorities and what I could be doing with my skills and experience. At this point, coming to work for you to use my personal and professional background to help other families work through difficult illnesses and the stresses they bring to their households seems like where I really belong.

Research the organization and its senior management, where they have been and where they wish to go. When your interviewer or the assistant calls to schedule the interview, request an annual report, a strategic plan, or other material that will shed more light on the organization. Ask, "Is there anything that you can provide me, which I can't easily download from your website, that might give me more information about your organization and allow me to show you how I can best help you achieve your goals?" Having a thorough understanding of the organization will help you better assess and, therefore, better communicate in the language of the nonprofit sector how they will benefit by bringing you on staff.

Likely Nonprofit Interview Questions

Before you step over the threshold of an interviewer's office, you had better be prepared to impress them with well-thought-out answers to questions you haven't yet heard. Most of their questions can be anticipated, but you should always be prepared for the unexpected.

The Good . . .

Good interview questions are insightful, forward-thinking questions that allow you to tie prospective achievements to a proven track record. Here are some examples:

- "Why are you interested in raising money for the spotted owl?"
- "What did you do at General Electric that has prepared you for the job of communications around homeless issues?"
- "How did you raise internal corporate morale, and will those ideas transfer to the city library system?"

By the time you step into the interviewer's office, your work history as presented on your résumé has already at least minimally qualified you for the job. Good interview questions focus both on the projects and programs you have managed as well as your hopes, dreams, and desires in this new position in this new sector. Employers are as much interested in what you have accomplished as in what it will be like to work with you on a daily basis.

Answer questions thoroughly, but succinctly, through stories that detail both your experience and your personal style. You should always answer the interviewer's questions, but the direction you take your answers is up to you. Make a list of the points you want to get across in the interview—how you originally got interested in the field, why you are making this sector switch right now, how your background and specific projects have prepared you for the position, how your passion is in line with the organization's mission, and how this position fits into your future career goals—and thread them throughout the answers you give to questions. Make sure to underscore constantly your belief in the mission of the nonprofit and your understanding of how this sector will be different from the corporate world you wish to leave behind.

The Bad . . .

Invariably, the interviewer will roll around to a "bad" interview question, one that you feel a bit timid about answering. It could be because you were fired, had a bad relationship with your boss, or didn't quite succeed in a job. It could even be as simple as asking pointedly about your sector switch and its likely success or failure. Some such questions might include:

- "So, you weren't in your last job for very long. What went wrong?"
- "You seem to move around a lot. Why?"
- "Tell me about a project that failed and your role in that failure?"

As much as you are tempted, jokes about poisoning your last boss aren't really funny, especially to someone who might be your next one. Everyone has spots on their résumé that don't shine as brightly as others. Don't attempt to cover them up. Making jokes or floundering through a long story will only make you look nervous, or worse, like you are lying. When confronted with a failure or a firing, just come clean.

Hit the incident head on. Say that you are glad that the interviewer brought it up. Relate that the situation was a difficult one and stick to the facts when describing it. You might even be able to use it as the reason that you tired of the corporate rat race and want to move into an organization worth the fight. Give an accurate but overall positive assessment of what went wrong and what you learned from the situation. Never, ever badmouth your former boss or old coworkers.

Finally, take blame where blame is due. Candidates who always point the finger anywhere but at themselves look as though they either cannot comprehend the problem or are covering up something. Turn the lens back onto yourself and use it as a chance to point out how you learn from your own mistakes. Nonprofits will appreciate your honesty and integrity and the fact that you can grow and change, because this sector switch will be a giant opportunity to succeed or fail doing just that.

. . . and the Ugly

Every so often an interviewer will stumble, whether intentionally or not, into illegal territory. Here are some ugly questions:

- "So, are you a native New Yorker, or are you not from around here?"

- "Travilani, is that an Italian name? My grandmother was Italian."

- "Will it be difficult on your family for you to begin traveling for work?"

Do these sound like illegal questions, or just small talk? Technically, they are illegal.

Illegal questions are questions related to your birthplace, nationality, native language or the ancestry of you, your spouse, your children, or your parents; your age; your sexual orientation or marital status; your race or color; your religion or the religious days or traditions you observe; any physical disabilities or handicaps you might have; an arrest record; your health or medical history; or your pregnancy or plans for pregnancy, birth control practices, and child care arrangements of you or your significant other.

While you aren't bound to answer these questions, you also do yourself a disservice by explaining to your interviewer the intricacies of employment law. Use your judgment before riding the politically correct bus out of town and away from your chances at a second interview. Most nonprofits can't afford to have a full-time human resources person interviewing all candidates, so your interviewer, while highly accomplished developing and implementing programs, is likely quite inexperienced and means no harm. A lecture from you only makes you appear rigid, possibly adding to the corporate stereotype. Instead, change the subject, and your green interviewer will get the picture. If, on the other hand, you sense that your interviewer is blatantly discriminating against you, you can and should call the interview to an end; it isn't a place you'd want to work anyway.

Ten Frequently Asked Nonprofit Interview Questions

Be prepared to answer these questions:

1. What can you do for our organization?

2. Of which accomplishment are you proudest?

3. And of which are you least?

4. What was the last argument you won, and how?

5. What is the first thing you would do in this position if it was offered to you today?

6. Tell me about yourself and what brings you here today?

7. Why are you leaving the corporate sector?

8. What do you do to relax in your spare time?

9. What will be your biggest challenge in this position? In coming to the nonprofit sector?

10. Why should we hire you instead of some of the others we are interviewing?

Speaking the Lingo

Before you head into the interview, review the section on language differences in Chapter 2. Take your cues from the nonprofit itself: some nonprofits are grassroots and old-school in their approach, while others are social enterprise models with full staffs of MBAs. Using the job description, website, and other promotional materials, such as annual reports, direct mail pieces, or grant applications, you can discern the specific language of this particular nonprofit.

Examples of Corporate Answers and Nonprofit Answers to the Same Question

Example #1: Have you had experience raising money?

- **Corporate answer.** Yes. I raised $10 million in venture capital for my last start-up endeavor. I see no reason why I can't raise the $2 million you need annually to run this program. Raising money is raising money, and I'm great at it.

- **Nonprofit answer.** Yes. I have had a great deal of experience raising capital in the corporate sector, and I have many transferable skills that would help me be successful raising money in the nonprofit sector. I know, of course, that raising $10 million in venture funds isn't the same, because my investors expected to make a lot of money in return, and in the nonprofit sector, the donors will get a different type of return—a great feeling of doing a good thing. But let me tell you what skills it took to raise that $10 million. First, I had to research my prospective investors. Second, I had to begin a relationship with them and build trust in the fact that I would be stewarding their money. Third, I had to determine when, how, and where to ask and for how much. Finally, I had to stay in constant contact with them throughout the life of that "gift" to ensure that they were satisfied, continually engaged, and possibly interested in giving more at a later date.

Example #2: Are you willing to roll up your sleeves and get your hands dirty?
- **Corporate answer.** Sure. I'm not afraid of hard work. I am often in the office late at night and early in the morning. I do whatever is needed to get the job done.

- **Nonprofit answer.** Yes. In fact, I understand that this organization has less support staff that I am used to, but let me tell you that just yesterday, I was the one changing the toner on the copier and refilling the paper trays. I feel no need to stand on ceremony because I am the boss. In fact, everyone in my shop pulls together to get the job done. We are all equal players when there is a task at hand or a deadline to be met.

Example #3: How have you determined whether or not a program or line of business is worth continuing?
- **Corporate answer.** Simply put, we have bottom-line goals. If the product is performing, we keep going. If not, we axe it and any staff who were responsible for its failure. I did that last month, making an example of the employee, and the rest of the staff has been working harder ever since.

- **Nonprofit answer.** Many factors go into a success or a failure, whether a lack of planning, poor execution, or a missed market. There are also different definitions of success. In August of last year, we had a product that was failing by our corporate standards of bottom-line numbers. I took the staff member aside and privately asked why he thought the failure was occurring. He told me that he wasn't able to manage a piece of it adequately and felt responsible. Instead of firing him, I decided to reward his honesty with some additional training. The product isn't failing anymore, but it's also not a runaway success. That being said, this employee has now come back with three other great ideas that have been tremendous successes, and the other staff have followed his example. I'm always willing to lose a little money in one area to gain a better, stronger, more invested staff all around. Plus, at the end of the day, we're even more profitable.

Phase Three: Tag, You're It!

At some point in the interview, usually about three quarters of the way through, you will be asked if you have any questions. It may seem like the moment when you can finally let out a sigh of relief, sit back, and revel in the fact that the evaluation is over. Don't fall into that trap. As a candidate, and especially as someone new to the sector, you will be judged by your questions as well as your answers.

Whoever said that there are no stupid questions never sat in on a job interview. There are plenty of stupid questions, and the candidates who ask them don't get offered jobs. If you ask no questions, you will have lost a unique opportunity to learn about the organization, not to mention getting labeled as having no intellectual curiosity or enthusiasm about the position or the organization.

Be Prepared with Questions

Bring along good questions, albeit not too many. Three to four is a good number; ask five if you must. You will be judged both on your intellectual savvy and your etiquette. Don't make the committee late for the next interview because you can't take hints like eye rolls, seat shifts, heavy clock glances, and monosyllabic answers—all of these actions indicate that the interview is over. If the interviewer likes you, you will have all the time in the world to ask follow-up questions as the process unfolds.

Focus your questions on the future of the organization rather than the organizational chart or the salary range. Asking nitpicky questions will only make the interviewer think you are a small thinker; there will be time for the details later, like when you are reviewing an offer. Plus, an overwhelming concern about salary or benefits only underscores that your first career was for personal profit and not service to the community.

Do Your Homework

Remember that brainy kid in junior high who asked questions like, "I did some extra reading and became curious. Can you tell me more about the crop rotation method of the early Mesopotamians?" We might not have learned our lesson then, but we can now. Curiosity and an active, lively intellect get attention. Every other student hated that kid, but the teacher always gave "the brain" an A+. By asking questions that show off your research or bring up strengths that the search committee might have overlooked, you can further impress a crowd that is still actively grading your performance.

Pull out the copy of the IRS Form 990 that you downloaded from the Internet (easily found and free at *www.guidestar.org*). Thumb through your dog-eared copy of the last annual report to discuss a program that you find particularly interesting. Mention something you saw in the last newsletter. Showing that you have taken the time to learn about the organization, whether by downloading information, discussing the organization with volunteers or board members, or through other research, will impress the search committee into believing that your sector switch is, indeed, motivated by all the right reasons.

The Pre-Interview Checklist

- [ ] An interview cheat sheet with achievements and explanations organized by job and function, easily digestible by someone in another sector

- [ ] An appointment book to schedule a follow-up interview on the spot

- [ ] A working watch to ensure early arrival

- [ ] A folder with five extra résumés, business cards, pen or paper, and a notepad

- [ ] Tissues or a handkerchief

- [ ] Directions to the interview location (easily found online)

- [ ] A portfolio of your creative work, strategic plans, or other proud accomplishments, preferably displaying anything you've done as a volunteer or board member

- [ ] A list of questions that show insight and research into the nonprofit sector and this particular organization and its challenges

- [ ] A silenced cell phone

- [ ] A copy of the job announcement, or notes taken about the position, to reread while you are waiting for the interview to begin. Circle nonprofit buzzwords to use throughout the interview.

- [ ] Breath mints

- [ ] A list of nonprofit references, if available, with current contact information and a brief explanation of their relationship to you or the project on which you worked together

- [ ] A sense of humor about yourself and humility about the challenges of switching sectors

- [ ] Letters of recommendation, preferably from nonprofit colleagues you've met along your journey

- [ ] A firm handshake, good eye contact, and a smile

Creativity Counts

By all means, ask questions on a variety of topics. Your search committee most likely has sat in the same chairs in the same room, listening to the same kind of candidates talk about the same sorts of subjects all day, and anything vaguely boring—like multiple questions on the same topic—will further lull them into a coma. Appearing somewhat knowledgeable but still intrigued about subjects interesting to each search committee member just might add that extra bit of enthusiasm necessary to catapult you ahead of One-Note Sally.

Good subjects to cover include the environment in which the organization operates, the management style employed by the top brass, obstacles and challenges that stand in the way of success, and the organization's view of its future. You can ask questions that highlight how you feel your corporate background will meld with the hopes and dreams of their leadership.

Force Interesting Answers

Avoid questions with obvious or readily available answers—like in the job description, for example—or questions that can be answered simply with a yes or a no. You can ask your interviewer for clarification on a specific point, but don't ask for a repeat explanation of an entire subject, or you will risk coming across as the candidate without any listening comprehension skills. Stay away from such unsavory topics as salary, benefits, and vacation time. Similarly, questions about weekend assignments, tuition reimbursements, pay schedules and Bring Your Dog to Work Day frequency should also be avoided. Asking such questions will paint your candidacy as more focused on what the organization can do for you than what you can do for it.

Great Questions That Show Your Understanding of the Nonprofit Sector

What are the main objectives and responsibilities of the position? Is a strategic plan already in place to meet them?

- How involved is the board, and how would you characterize it?

- What challenges or obstacles are commonly encountered in reaching these objectives?

- What is the desired time frame for reaching the objectives?

- What resources are available internally, and what must be found or raised elsewhere to reach the objectives?

- How would you characterize the management philosophy of this organization? Of your department?

- What strengths and weaknesses currently exist in the staff that will report to me?

- How has this organization changed in the past, and where does it expect to go in the future?

- What is the top priority of the person who accepts this job? How will the successful candidate be judged in 6–12 months?

- What are the next steps in the selection process?

The Interview's Over: Now What?

With an ounce of relief and a pound of pride, you step from your interviewer's office exhilarated that you have made it through yet another step of the job search process. But any good candidate knows that the job interview doesn't end with, "Thanks, we'll be in touch." So what do you do now?

As you exit the interview, and undoubtedly throughout the ride home, you will begin to find yourself hounded by pesky thoughts of things you forgot to say. Resist the urge to pick up the phone and call your interviewer; until a decision has been made, everything you say can and will be held against you. You may come up with other things you wish to say, and calling each time will only make you look scatterbrained. But the nonprofit sector is a little kinder to mistakes and more forgiving of personal foibles. Returning to your interviewer with some thoughts about the interview is not only acceptable, it is encouraged—as long as you follow the right form.

Carefully debrief the interview. Think through the questions that were asked and the questions that were not asked. Review the list of points you expected to make and weigh them against what actually came out of your mouth. Judge your performance and think through what you could improve upon next time. Every performance can be improved, and until you accept a position, you should always assume there will be another.

Thank-You Notes Are Key

Regrettably, the art of the personalized thank-you note is a lost one. In the age of electronic communication, it's rare for hiring managers to get thank-you notes from candidates they have interviewed. When they do, it seems that most are quick notes jotted hastily, with typos throughout, and sent electronically without much effort or thought at all. Hiring managers would like to think that your interest in the job at hand, not to mention your respect for their time, warrants more than that.

A personalized thank-you note is not just polite, it's an opportunity for you to give one last sales pitch, and it's a chance to fill in the hiring manager on anything you realize you forget to say in the interview. Yet most candidates forswear this golden opportunity. A good thank-you note doesn't gush; it expresses both appreciation for the hiring manager's time as well as a forgotten—or repeated—clarification of your skills and experiences as they relate to the organization's needs and challenges. A thank-you note gets their attention, and a good one gets placed in the résumé book and is ultimately read, and duly noted, by the search committee. As a sector switcher, this is the ideal moment for you to underscore your knowledge of this more touchy-feely world, showing how well you can and will fit into it.

Grace Jobseeker
123 Highway One
Newton, Massachusetts 02458
(617) 555-4658

Dear Jane Headmistress:

Thank you for spending time with me this afternoon discussing the exciting position at Newton Montessori School. As I explained, I feel that my skills and experiences crafting brands and marketing for The Major Corporation, combined with my ten years as a parent of Montessori children, will enable me to serve the school as an excellent director of admissions and recruiting.

I was extremely impressed with the work that the school has already done to position itself among its peers as a leader among other Montessori schools in the greater Boston area. As you know, I believe that what Newton Montessori needs at this time is to be "branded" with potential incoming parents of younger children as well as to neighborhood private schools for outgoing sixth graders. By becoming "the school from which the best kids graduate," Newton Montessori will have a waiting list in no time, making the job of selecting students a difficult but enviable task. As we discussed, my background in creating brands around education-based products, specifically for this age group and sector, make me an ideal candidate to develop the Newton Montessori brand.

In our interview, I told you a good deal about the work that I did on the communications committee of our parent guild. I forgot to mention, however, that the school that our sons attended is still, five years later, using the materials I helped developed and speaks of them with great acclaim. In creating them, I aimed for timelessness, knowing that the school wouldn't have the budget to recreate materials each year. It gives me great pleasure to know that what I created has been so effective.

While I understand that you will need to see other candidates, I want to be clear that I am actively seeking new employment and have several interviews scheduled for next week. This position is the one in which I am most interested, however, and I will be checking back with you at the end of next week to see if you have made any determinations about your decision-making time line. I would consider it an honor and a privilege to be able to serve in this wonderful school.

Warm regards,
Grace JobSeeker

Post-Interview Reflections

After you leave the interview, it is essential to debrief about your performance. Answers to these questions will inform your thank-you note as well as future interview performance:

- Did you feel comfortable in the interview?

- Which questions could you have answered better?

- Where did you succeed? Where did you fail?

- Which topics led to awkward silences?

- Did you emphasize your understanding of the connection between the organization's needs and your skills and experiences?

- Did you create a conversational atmosphere?

- Did the interviewer ask questions for which you were not prepared?

- Did you understand and address the interviewer's concerns about your candidacy given your corporate background?

- Did you forget to ask any questions about the job or organization that would inform you decision should the job be offered to you?

- What would you differently next time?

Handling the Follow-Up Call Well

Any conversation with a headhunter or hiring manager after an interview may contain an offer. Many will include reconnaissance questions necessary so that when an offer does come, it will be accepted. Like a proposal of marriage, a job offer is a question rarely asked without full knowledge of the response. Yet because your sector switch presents different issues around compensation, more questions likely will be asked of you than of other candidates.

Keep a list handy of any remaining questions you have about the position or the organization. You would need to satisfy any concerns before accepting a job anyway, so asking them during follow-up calls gives you more control over the conversation. Don't feel pressured into answering questions if you are surprised by the call. The headhunter doesn't know your schedule and can't see that you are sitting in your living room waiting all day for the air conditioner service technician. Put off the call with an excuse of a meeting currently in progress to give yourself time to catch your breath and call back when you are calm, collected, and, yes, cool.

Strategic References

Once you've mastered the interview, it's quickly on to the reference-checking stage of the search. You may be asked for these references at the interview or soon thereafter, so it's a good idea to have them prepped and ready.

Think of your references as an extension of your interview. Rather than your telling the search committee, again, how great you would be at this job, your references will do it for you. Be sure to choose references who can talk about the great work you've done with them in the context of your work in the nonprofit sector. If your references can only talk about your corporate prowess, they won't help you and may even hurt you. Because you'll need some references that can talk about your day job try, if possible, to pick people who have done some nonprofit volunteering—either with you or on their own—and can talk intelligently about how you would overcome any potential challenges.

Prepping Your References

Ask your references for permission before you list them. Prepare each by providing a current copy of your résumé, the job description, and some information about the organization. If appropriate, remind them about some of the exceptional things you did together that set you up for success in this new role.

Don't be too prescriptive about talking points, but remind them that this is a sector switch for you and they may get some specific questions about how you would make that leap. Make sure they know why you think you would be right in this new position. Allow your references to ask any questions they have so that they can they can process this move with you, not with the headhunter.

Handling a Likely Negative Reference

At some point in the process, a good hiring manager will ask if there is anyone they cannot call. These are the "off-list" references, and any one of them might dredge up some bad news. If you know that something is coming—perhaps you are quitting your current job because your boss is horrible and no one leaves the department well—make sure you are honest with the hiring manager. Hearing bad news from you will usually inoculate you against any issues that may arise; not hearing it from you will make you look as though you were purposefully evasive and lessen your credibility throughout the rest of the process.

If there is something more serious—a criminal record, a failed credit rating, or a college degree not actually earned for example—fess up immediately. Because nonprofits steward public money, they are often under high levels of public scrutiny. To that end, many nonprofits insist on criminal, credit, and educational background checks by any number of private firms who do this sort of thing. They will find out what you are hoping to hide, and your only chance of inoculating yourself is to come out with it first and share the relevant context, rehabilitation, or remorse.

Thanking Your References

If you are searching for a job, your references most likely will get called several times at potentially inconvenient moments to laud your greatness. Keep them energized and engaged by actively appreciating them. Rather than sending an unnecessary gift, thank them with a note that updates them on your job search progress. Do not ask them if they were contacted—because they normally would be promised confidentiality by the recruiter—but they may still tell you. Either way, thank all of your references when the search ends, whether or not you get the job.

Conclusion

Writing a cover letter will seem, at first, like a daunting and overwhelming task. You'll need to learn a different tone from what you've used in cover letters you've written throughout your corporate career. However, writing it in your own voice will become more comfortable with practice and eventually will seem like second nature. So, too, will your interview performance. As with anything else, practice makes perfect, so start talking to everyone and don't stop until you've landed your next job. Your references are a perfect sounding board, because they'll both need to know why you are making this move and why you think you are qualified to do so. They believe in you, have seen your career in action, and are willing to help. Let them—they'll thank you for it.

Testimonials from Successful Career Changers:

Jennifer Keys, *Director of Human Resources*,
Institute for Systems Biology, Seattle, Washington

Jennifer started her career working in marketing for a scientific instrument manufacturer, but something wasn't gelling. "One day my boss pulled me aside and told me, 'Jennifer, you're doing a good job, but this really just isn't for you.'" At her suggestion, Jennifer made a move into human resources. After relocating to Seattle, she landed a job in human resources at a biotechnology start-up. She stayed in the corporate world for six more years, and while she loved the substance of the work itself, she found the "hire, discipline, terminate, hire" grind was making her incredibly unhappy. When she saw an ad for a human resources position at Girl Scouts, "This star lit up and the planets aligned, and I knew I had to have this job."

Still, Jennifer faced some difficulty in her transition. "When nonprofits have some extra money, they use it to hire another fundraiser or program person, not a human resources specialist," she explains. "While nonprofits are excellent at training staff and volunteers around certain activities," Jennifer found that, "In other ways, human resources in many nonprofits is about 15 years behind. The culture is also completely alien to anyone raised in corporate America. There is a learning curve."

Jennifer left the Girl Scouts when she had done all she felt she could for the organization. However, she chose to find her next role in the nonprofit sector as well, this time for a larger nonprofit. She continues to enjoy the challenge and enjoyment, although she hasn't yet found a better work-life balance. "Employees in nonprofits are spread very thin," she explains. "Yet, seeing a girl go camping for the first time or facilitating the hire of a scientist whose discovery will change the face of health care makes it all worthwhile."

How did Jennifer convince the Girl Scouts that she was driven by their mission?

Having been a Girl Scout for much of her youth, Jennifer dug out her old Girls Scouts sash and brought it to the interview. While she would never have done such a thing in the private sector, she gambled correctly that the Girl Scouts would love it. "Something like that," she explains, "is not only acceptable in the nonprofit world, it's encouraged!" Jennifer took a pay cut to work at the Girl Scouts but still considers it the best move of her career.

What differences did Jennifer find between human resources work in corporate companies and nonprofit organizations?

Jennifer found that she had to change her focus completely when entering the nonprofit sector. "Employees are working for less than market rate and expect some other types of compensation," she explains. "I had to get used to consensus decision making, left-of-center employees, and conversations about things like disadvantaged groups under American imperialism. If you think you are a liberal, think again." Jennifer also had to get accustomed to employees who gave countless unpaid hours to the organization and, in return, expected her to overlook failings from time to time.

How did Jennifer acclimate to the more casual nonprofit culture?

In her previous corporate jobs, Jennifer did not experience the level of personal camaraderie found in the nonprofit sector. "My corporate background did not prepare me for the openness I found in this sector," she explains, "and so I had to learn to check some of my reserve at the door, lest my co-workers brand me as too politically correct or too corporate."

Jennifer's Key Lessons Learned:

- ✓ "Employees in the nonprofit sector demand transparency. If they are working for 30 percent less than market, they expect to have not just a say but a vote. Decisions are often based on relationships, not just facts and figures."
- ✓ "The culture has to fit you. While the eccentricities of some staff might make you a teeny bit crazy at times, it is part of the fabric that makes this sector so rich."
- ✓ "Be yourself, your whole self, in the interview. Read about the organization, be prepared to ask smart questions, and show them how your skills—and your passion—make you the right hire."

Ellise M. LaMotte, *Project Director,*
Women of Ethnic Diversity Initiative, The Commonwealth Institute
Boston, Massachusetts

Ellise landed in the nonprofit sector completely by accident. "I had gone to school and studied engineering," Ellise says, "and went right to work at New England Telecom, which then became Verizon, which spun off Genuity, and so the roller coaster went." By the time Verizon had decided against buying back Genuity, Ellise had already made contingency plans by getting her real estate license. When the layoff came, she was prepared. "I had set off on my real estate adventure," she says, "and after a couple of years, decided to have another adventure: motherhood."

Ellise settled into her new life but began to ask herself if she really wanted to stay home all day with her six-month-old baby. "I missed hearing people say, 'Job well done!' at the end of the day," she says, "but I knew I didn't want to go back into big corporate America again. If I was going to be away from my baby, I didn't want to be putting in a circuit for a telecom company, but doing something that really matters." That's when one of her friends sent Ellise an announcement for a position as project director for a nonprofit enabling diverse women entrepreneurs to grow their business ventures. "The job was networking and helping others succeed," she says, "which was what I had always enjoyed doing most in my professional and personal lives, plus it was working for a women's nonprofit, so I knew it would be family friendly."

What surprised Ellise most when she started her nonprofit job?

I kind of knew that nonprofits were different," she says, "but I didn't know how different they were." Ellise quickly realized that nonprofits were less hierarchical than corporations where. "Everyone does everything—from moving boxes to making coffee—and no one wastes money," she says. She was also impressed with the numbers of power players she was exposed to on her very first day. "The women I meet with on a daily basis are on the largest boards, run the most successful companies, and are elected to some of the highest offices in the state," she says. "It's amazing to sit in a room with several hundred million dollars of net worth, especially when they are all women!"

How has motherhood affected Ellise's professional life?

At the end of the day, Ellise realized that the difference in culture, acceptance, and access only added a layer to what was already a viable business plan. "Going back to work after having my baby was harder for me than the transition from corporate to nonprofit," she says. "This is a nonprofit, but we still have revenue targets." That added layer, though, made all the difference for Ellise as a new mother. "This nonprofit is much friendlier to me as a mother than my corporate-America experience would have been," she says. "No one is giving me the evil eye when I have to leave early, and no one thinks twice when I have to work from home because my child is sick."

Ellise's Key Lessons Learned:

✓ "'Nonprofit' doesn't mean 'no money.' If you find the right nonprofit, it will be every bit as businesslike as you have come to enjoy in your corporate life, but with the heart you didn't know you missed."

✓ "Network with the nonprofits where you want to work. If they are small, they might not have jobs when you first start looking, but as soon as a job opens up, you'll be the first one they call."

✓ "As you are interviewing, don't be afraid of having conversations about your personal schedule and how it might affect your work. You'll be surprised that nonprofits will understand where you are coming from and won't make you feel like you are begging for permission to have a life outside of the office."

EPILOGUE

Throughout this book, you've read the stories of people who have made the transition from the corporate to the nonprofit sector. Some came by accident; others were more purposeful. All are thrilled with their decision, and most wished they had done it sooner.

Undoubtedly you picked up *Mission Driven* because you were curious about what working in the nonprofit sector would mean for you, personally, professionally, and financially. This book endeavored to help answer those questions and inspire you on your journey. Now you are ready—go follow your dream!

ABOUT THE AUTHOR

Laura Gassner Otting has spent the last 20 years working to strengthen organizations that weave our social and civic fabric. More than half of that time has been as the CEO of Nonprofit Professionals Advisory Group, a firm she founded to ensure that all nonprofits, regardless of their budget size and geographic footprint, had access to the most effective methods of securing that all important resource of talent. Over the past 11 years, she and her team have placed hundreds of leaders in nonprofits with budgets from $250,000 to $450,000,000, in the United States and around the world.

Prior to founding the Nonprofit Professionals Advisory Group in 2002, Laura helped build the start-up ExecSearches.com, a leading website for mid- to senior-level nonprofit job postings, and served as a vice president at Isaacson, Miller, one of the most highly respected nonprofit executive search firms in the country. Previously, Laura served as a presidential appointee for the White House Office of National Service and a program officer for the Corporation for National and Community Service where she was part of the team that created AmeriCorps, and as a member of the Clinton/Gore Transition Team and 1992 Election Team. Laura holds a Master of Arts in Political Management from the George Washington University and a Bachelor of Arts in Government from the University of Texas at Austin.

Laura serves on the boards of College Bound Dorchester, the Eli J. Segal Citizen Leadership Program at Brandeis University, and Newton Montessori School. She is a founding board member of SheGives, a philanthropy marketplace catalyzing support for a broad range of philanthropies around Boston. She has served as a member of the board of Camp Starfish and the Alumni Board of the Graduate School of Political Management at the George Washington University and as the founding board chair of both Strong Women, Strong Girls and the Boston Choral Ensemble. Laura is a curator for TedxBeaconStreet in Boston. Always up for a challenge, Laura completed the 2012, 2014 Boston and 2012 Chicago Marathons, in all cases, raising significant money for charities.

Laura is the author of *Change Your Career: Transitioning to the Nonprofit Sector* and is widely quoted for her expertise in mission-driven work in publications like *The New York Times*, *The Chronicle of Philanthropy* and *Money* magazine.

ACKNOWLEDGMENTS

The original manuscript of this book could not have been written without the help and support of so many friends, colleagues, and loved ones. Heaping mounds of gratitude go to Linda Babcock, Jack Goldsmith, Leslie Williams, Jameila Haddawi, Elizabeth Shreve, Jess Brooks, Amy Goldstein, Mark Miller, Caren and Jon Krumerman, Walter and Shelly Gassner, and Butch and Barbara Otting for helping me launch this project and for their sage wisdom, relentless support, and unending patience throughout. Special appreciation belongs to the editors at Kaplan Publishing who asked me to write that first publication; and to Makeba Greene and Jessica Cook, rock star researchers from Nonprofit Professionals Advisory Group, and the fine folks at Elevate, who helped me make it current once more. Mostly, though, I remain in debt to my children, Ben and Toby, who every day inspire me to make the world a better place, and to my husband, Jon, my wings and my safety net, who always remains my true north.

APPENDIX

This abridged list should give you a sense of the resources at your disposal as you make this transition into the nonprofit sector. A longer, more detailed list may be found at http://www.Nonprofitprofessionals.com.

Job Boards by Interest Area

General Nonprofit Job Websites
American Society of Association Executives –http://www.asaecenter.org/
Bridgestar – http://www.bridgestar.org
CEO Update – http://www.associationjobs.com
Chronicle of Philanthropy –http://philanthropy.com/jobs/
ExecSearches.com – http://www.execsearches.com
Guidestar – http://www.guidestar.org
Idealist – http://www.idealist.org
Nonprofit Oyster – http://www.Nonprofitoyster.com
Nonprofit Times – http://www.nptimes.com
Opportunity NOCs –http://www.opportunityNOCS.org

Academia, Teaching, and Higher Education
CASE – http://www.case.org
Chronicle of Higher Education –http://www.chronicle.com
Council for Special Education –http://www.specialedcareers.org/
Education Week – http://www.agentk–12.org
Higher Ed Jobs – http://www.higheredjobs.com

Animals and the Environment
American Zoo and Aquarium Association Positions –http://www.aza.org/JobListings/
Environmental Careers and Opportunities –http://www.ecojobs.com
EnviroJobs – EnviroJobs@yahoogroups.com
Environmental Jobs and Careers –http://www.ejobs.org/
Green Dream Jobs –http://www.sustainablebusiness.com/jobs/

Arts and Cultural
Arts Jobs – http://www.artjob.org
Arts Wire – http://www.artswire.org
Museum Jobs – http://www.museumjobs.org

Foundations and Philanthropy
Council on Foundations – http://www.cof.org
The Foundation Center with the Philanthropy News
Digest – http://www.fdncenter.org
On Philanthropy Job Bank –http://www.dotorgjobs.com/rt/dojhome
PNN Online – http://pnnonline.org/

Health and Medical
Health Careers Online –http://www.healthcareers–online.com
Health Career Web – http://www.healthcareerweb.com
Public Health Employment Connection –http://cfusion.sph.emory.edu/PHEC/phec.cfm

International
International Jobs – http://www.internationaljobs.org
Overseas Jobs – http://www.overseasjobs.org
U.S. Foreign Service – http://www.state.gov

Legal

American Bar Associations – http://www.abanet.org

Emplawyer – http://Emplawyer.net

LawJobs – http://www.LawJobs.com

Lesbian, Gay, Bisexual and Transgender

Diversity Working – http://www.diversityworking.com/career/Non_Profit/gay_lesbians.htm

GLP Careers – http://www.glpcareers.com/

ProGayJobs – http://www.progayjobs.com/Nonprofit.php

Queer Jobs Listserv – queerjobs@yahoogroups.com

National and Community Service

Community Career Center –http://www.Nonprofitjobs.org

Idealist – http://www.idealist.org

Lifetime of Service (AmeriCorps Alums) –http://www.lifetimeofservice.org/networking/

VISTAnet – listserv@listserv.icors.org

Politics, Organizing and Government

Careers in Government –http://www.careersingovernment.com

National Organizers Alliance Job Bank –http://www.ultrabit.net/noa/jobbank.cfm

Opportunities in Public Affairs – http://brubach.com

Union Jobs Clearinghouse – http://www.unionjobs.com

Religious Organizations

Christian Jobs Listserv –christian–jobs@yahoogroups.com

Jewish Communal Jobs Clearinghouse –http://www.jewishjobs.com

Ministry Connect – http://www.ministryconnect.org

Work Ministry – http://www.workministry.com

Social Service

Coalition for Human Needs –http://www.chn.org/jobs/index.html

Jobs in Fair Housing – http://www.fairhousing.com

Social Service Jobs – http://www.socialservice.com

National Association of Social Workers JobLink –http://www.naswdc.org

Technology

Contract Employment Weekly, Jobs Online – http://www.cjhunter.com

Nonprofit Tech Jobs – http://groups.yahoo.com/group/Nonprofit_Tech_Jobs

Dice.com – http://www.dice.com

Women

Career Women – http://www.careerwomen.com/

Feminist Majority Career Center –http://www.feminist.org

Women's Information Network –http://www.winonline.org

Executive Search Firms Serving the Nonprofit Sector

Auerbach Associates – http://www.auerbach–assc.com

Commongood Careers – http://www.cgcareers.org

Development Resource Group – http://www.drg.com

Diversified Search – http://www.divsearch.com

Egmont and Associates –http://www.egmontassociates.com

Isaacson, Miller – http://www.imsearch.com

Kittleman & Associates, LLC – http://www.kittleman.com

Korn Ferry – http://www.kornferry.com

Lois Lindauer Searches – http://www.lllsearches.com

Morris & Berger – http://www.morrisberger.com

Nonprofit Professionals Advisory Group –http://www.Nonprofitprofessionals.com

Russell Reynolds Associates, Inc. –http://www.russellreynolds.com

Slesinger Management –http://www.slesingermanagement.com

Spencer Stuart – http://www.spencerstuart.com

Appendix

Temp/Staffing Agencies Making Placements in Nonprofits
Accounting Management Solutions –http://www.amsolutions.net
Careers for Causes – http://www.placementpros.com/
First Source Staffing – http://fssny.com
Professionals for Nonprofits – http://www.nonprofitstaffing.com
Nonprofit Staffing Solutions – http://www.nonprofittemps.com/

Continued Reading
Books on Nonprofit Management
The Nonprofit Sector: A Research Handbook, by Walter W. Powell and Richard Steinberg, Yale University Press; 2nd Edition (November 1, 2006)
The Nature of the Nonprofit Sector by J. Steven Ott, Westview Press (October 1, 2000)
Good to Great and the Social Sector: A Monograph to Accompany Good to Great, Jim Collins, HarperCollins (November 30, 2005)
Love and Profit, James A. Autry, Harper Paperbacks; Reprint edition (September 1, 1992)
Leadership in Nonprofit Organizations: Lessons from the Third Sector, Barry Dym and Harry Hutson, Sage Publications, Inc (January 12, 2005)

Books with Inspirational Stories
The Cathedral Within, by Billy Shore, Random House Trade Paperbacks (November 1, 2001)
Leaving Microsoft to Change the World, by John Wood, Collins (August 29, 2006)
How to Change the World, by David Bornstein, Oxford University Press, USA (February 5, 2004)
Be the Change! Change the World. Change Yourself. Edited by Michelle Nunn, Hundreds of Heads Books (November 1, 2006)
Encore: How Baby Boomers Are Inventing the Next Stage of Work, by Marc Freedman, PublicAffairs (May 30, 2007)

Magazines, Periodicals, and Journals
Alliance Insight – http://www.allianceonline.org/insights.ipage
Chronicle of Higher Education – http://www.chronicle.com
Chronicle of Philanthropy – http://www.philanthropy.com
Contributions Magazine – http://www.contributionsmagazine.com
Exempt Magazine – http://www.exemptmagazine.com/
Fast Company – http://www.fastcompany.com
Generocrity – http://www.generocitymag.com
Good Magazine – http://www.goodmagazine.com/
Nonprofit Quarterly – http://www.Nonprofitquarterly.org/
Nonprofit Times – http://www.nptimes.com
Stanford Social Innovation Review –http://www.ssireview.org/

E–Newsletters
Bridgestar – http://www.bridgestar.org
Case Foundation – http://www.casefoundation.org/about/contact/email–updates
Charity Channel – http://charitychannel.com/enewsletters/ncr/index.asp
Compass Point's Board Cafe – http://www.compasspoint.org/boardcafe/index.php
Just Give – http://www.justgive.org/html/Nonprofits/npnewsletter.html
Nonprofit About.com – http://Nonprofit.about.com/gi/pages/mmail.htm
Nonprofit Legal Issues – http://www.Nonprofitissues.com/
Nonprofit News Online – http://news.gilbert.org/
Nonprofit Policy News – http://www.ncna.org/index.cfm?fuseaction=Page.viewPage&pageId=696
Nonprofit Professionals Advisory Group –http://www.Nonprofitprofessionals.com
Omidyar Network – http://www.omidyar.net/home/
Skoll Foundation – http://www.skollfoundation.org/

Helpful Websites for Additional Research
Charity Navigator – http://www.charitynavigator.org
Guidestar – http://www.guidestar.org
National Center for Charitable Statistics – http://nccs.urban.org
Network for Good – http://www.networkforgood.org
The Nonprofit FAQs – http://www.nonprofits.org

Educational Resources:
Degrees or Concentrations in Nonprofit

Graduate Programs (Graduate Degrees)

The following schools offer programs where you can earn your Master of Arts (MA), Master of Business Administration (MBA), Master of Nonprofit Administration, (MNA), Master of Public Administration (MPA), Master of Public Policy (MPP), Master of Science (MS), or Doctor of Philosophy (PhD) in nonprofit management.

Alabama

Auburn University at Montgomery, MPA with Concentration Nonprofit

Arizona

Arizona State University, MPA in NonprofitManagement
University of Arizona, MPA in Nonprofits and Government

California

University of San Francisco, MNA
University of California at Los Angeles, MPP in Nonprofit Policy
San Francisco State University, MPA in Nonprofit Administration
University of San Diego, MA in Nonprofit Leadership and Management Studies
University of Southern California, MPA and MPP with Concentrations in Nonprofit Management

Colorado

Regis University, MNA
University of Colorado at Denver, MPA, Doctor of Philosophy in Public Administration

Connecticut

University of Connecticut, MPA with Concentration in Nonprofit Management
Yale University, MBA with Concentration in Nonprofit Management

District of Columbia

Georgetown University, MPA in Nonprofit Policy and Leadership
The George Washington University, MPA and MPP with Concentrations in Nonprofit Management

Delaware

University of Delaware, MA and MPA with Concentrations in Community Development and Nonprofit Leadership

Florida

Florida Atlantic University, MNA

Georgia

Georgia State University, MPA in Nonprofit Studies, MS in Urban Policy Studies in Nonprofit Studies
Kennesaw State University, MPA in Community Services/Nonprofit Administration
University of Georgia, MA in Nonprofit Organizations

Iowa

University of Northern Iowa, MA in Philanthropy and Nonprofit Development, MPP in Nonprofits

Illinois

DePaul University, MS in Public Service Management with Concentrations in Association and   Management, MS in Public Service Management in Fundraising and Philanthropy, MS in Public Service Management in Nonprofit Administration
Northwestern University, Master of Nonprofit Management
Southern Illinois University at Edwardsville, MPA
Illinois Institute of Technology, MPA in Nonprofit Management

Indiana

Indiana University at Bloomington, MPA and PhD with Concentrations in Nonprofit Management
Indiana University, Center on Philanthropy, MA in Philanthropic Studies, MPA in Nonprofit Management, PhD in Philanthropic Studies
Indiana University-Purdue University at Indianapolis, MPA in Nonprofit Management
University of Notre Dame, MS in Nonprofit Leadership

Appendix

Louisiana

Louisiana State University at Shreveport, MS in Human Services Administration

Maine

Clark University, MPA in Nonprofit Administration

Maryland

College of Notre Dame of Maryland, MA in Nonprofit Management

Johns Hopkins University, MA in Policy Studies in Nonprofit Sector

University of Maryland, University College, MA in Management in Nonprofit Management

Massachusetts

Harvard University, MPP, MPA, PhD in Public Policy / Public Administration

Lesley College, MBA in Not-for-Profit Management

Tufts University, MA in Nonprofit Organizations

Worcester State College, MS in Nonprofit Management

Michigan

Oakland University, MPA in Nonprofit Organization and Management

University of Michigan, MSW, MPA, MPP with Concentrations in Nonprofit Management

Wayne State University, Master of Interdisciplinary Studies in Nonprofit Sectors

Western Michigan University, MPA in Nonprofit Management and Leadership

Minnesota

St. Cloud State University, MS in Public and Nonprofit Institutions

University of Minnesota, Humphrey Institute, Master of Public Affairs in Nonprofits, Master of Management in Nonprofits

Missouri

University of Missouri at Kansas City, MPA in Nonprofit Management, Doctor of Philosophy in Public Administration in Nonprofit Management

University of Missouri at St. Louis, MPP in Nonprofit Management and Leadership

North Carolina

High Point University, MPA in Nonprofit Organizations

University of North Carolina at Greensboro, Master of Public Affairs in Nonprofit Management

Nebraska

University of Nebraska at Omaha, MPA in Nonprofit, Doctor of Philosophy in Public Administration in Nonprofit

New Jersey

Seton Hall University, MPA in Nonprofit Management

Kean University, MPA in Nonprofit Management

New York

CUNY - Baruch College, MPA in Nonprofit Administration

Long Island University, MPA in Not-for-Profit Management

New School University, MS in Nonprofit Management

New York University - Wagner Graduate School, MPA and Doctor of Philosophy with Specializations in Public and Nonprofit Management and Policy,

Management of International Public Service Organizations, and Nonprofit and NGOs

Ohio

Case Western Reserve University, MNA, Executive Doctor of Management

Cleveland State University, MA in Nonprofit Management, Doctor of Philosophy in Nonprofit Management

Kent State University, MBA in Nonprofit Management, MPA in Nonprofit Management

Ohio State University, Master of Social Work in Social Administration Practice

The Union Institute, MA in Nonprofit Management, PhD in Nonprofit Management

Oregon

Portland State University - Division of Public Administration, MPA in Nonprofit, Doctor of Philosophy in Public Administration and Policy in Nonprofit

University of Oregon, Master of Community & Regional Planning, MPA, Graduate Certificate in Not-for-Profit Management

Pennsylvania

Eastern University, MS in Nonprofit Management

Indiana University of Pennsylvania, Mater of Arts in Sociology in Administration & Evaluation and Human Services Administration, Doctor of Philosophy in Administration and Leadership Studies in Administration & Evaluation and Human Services Administration

Widener University, MPA in Nonprofit Administration

South Carolina

College of Charleston, MPA in Nonprofit Administration

South Dakota

University of South Dakota, MPA in Nonprofit Administration

Tennessee

University of Memphis, MPA in Nonprofit Administration

University of Tennessee, Chattanooga, MPA in Nonprofit Management

Texas

University of Houston – Victoria, MA in Interdisciplinary Studies in Nonprofit Leadership

University of Texas at Austin, Lyndon B. Johnson School of Public Affairs, MPA, PhD in Public Policy

University of Dallas, MBA in Nonprofit Management, MS in Management in Nonprofit Management

Virginia

George Mason University, MPA in Nonprofit Management

Virginia Commonwealth University, MPA in Nonprofit Management

Vermont

School for International Training, Program in Intercultural Service, Leadership, and Management (PIM) in Mission Driven Organizations

Washington

Seattle University, Executive Master of Not-For-Profit Leadership, MPA in Nonprofit Leadership

Wisconsin

University of Wisconsin – Milwaukee, MA, MBA, MPA in Nonprofit Management

Certificate Programs (Graduate Programs)

Alabama

Auburn University at Montgomery, Nonprofit Management and Leadership Certificate

University of Alabama at Birmingham, Graduate Certificate in Nonprofit Management

Arkansas

University of Arkansas at Little Rock, Graduate Certificate in Nonprofit Management

California

California State University – Hayward, Nonprofit Management Certificate

University of San Diego, Certificate in Nonprofit Leadership & Management

Calstate East Bay, Certificate in Nonprofit Management

Colorado

University of Colorado at Colorado Springs, Certificate in Nonprofit Management

Connecticut

University of Connecticut, Graduate Certificate in Nonprofit Management

Appendix

District of Columbia
> The George Washington University, Graduate Certificate in Nonprofit Management

Florida
> Florida Atlantic University, Nonprofit Management Executive Certificate

Georgia
> Georgia State University, Graduate Certificate in Nonprofit Management
> University of Georgia, Graduate Certificate in Nonprofit Organizations

Illinois
> DePaul University, Administrative Foundations Certificate, Nonprofit Leadership Certificate
> Southern Illinois University at Edwardsville, Non-Profit Management Certificate
> Illinois Institute of Technology, Certificate in Nonprofit Management
> Loyola University Chicago, Certificate of Advanced Study in Philanthropy
> Saint Xavier University, Certificate in Public and Non-Profit Management

Indiana
> Indiana University – Bloomington, Nonprofit Management Certificate
> Indiana University, Center on Philanthropy, Philanthropic Studies Certificate, Nonprofit Management Certificate
> Purdue University, Certificate in Nonprofit Management
> Perdue University North Central, Certificate in Nonprofit Management

Maryland
> College of Notre Dame of Maryland, Certificate in Leadership of Nonprofit Organizations
> Johns Hopkins University, Certificate in Nonprofit Studies
> University of Maryland, University College, Nonprofit Financial Management Certificate

Massachusetts
> Tufts University, Management of Community
> Organizations Certificate

Michigan
> Oakland University, Post-Master's Certificate in Nonprofit Organization & Management
> University of Michigan, Certificate in Nonprofit Management in Development
> Ferris State University, Philanthropic Studies Certificate
> Grand Valley State University, Graduate Certificate in Nonprofit Leadership
> Lawrence Technological University, Graduate Certificate in Nonprofit Management and Leadership
> Wayne State University, Master of Interdisciplinary Studies in Nonprofit Sectors
> Western Michigan University, Nonprofit Leadership Certificate

Minnesota
> University of Minnesota, Humphrey Institute, Nonprofit Management Certificate

Missouri
> University of Missouri at Kansas City, Fund Raising Certificate
> University of Missouri at St. Louis, Nonprofit Management and Leadership Certificate

New Jersey
> Seton Hall University, Certificate in Nonprofit Organization Management
> Rutgers University – Newark, Certificate in Nonprofit Management

New York
> Roberts Wesleyan College, Certificate in Nonprofit Leadership
> C.W. Post College, Nonprofit Management Advanced Certificate
> SUNY College at Brockport, Certificate in Nonprofit Management

Nevada
> University of Nevada, Certificate in Nonprofit Management

North Carolina

North Carolina State University, Graduate Certificate in Nonprofit Management

University of North Carolina – Greensboro, Nonprofit Management Certificate

University of North Carolina at Chapel Hill, Nonprofit Leadership Certificate

University of North Carolina at Chapel Hill, Social Work, Nonprofit Leadership Certificate

Ohio

Case Western Reserve University, Certificate in Nonprofit Management

Cleveland State University, Certificate in Nonprofit Management

University of Akron, Certificate in Nonprofit Management

Oregon

Portland State University - Division of Public Administration, Nonprofit Management Certificate, Nonprofit Development Certificate, Nonprofit Financial Management Certificate, Volunteer Management Certificate

University of Oregon, Graduate Certificate in Not-for-Profit Management

Pennsylvania

University of Pennsylvania, Certificate in Nonprofit Administration

University of Pittsburgh, Nonprofit Management Certificate

Widener University, Certificate of Advanced Graduate Studies in Nonprofit Management

Rhode Island

Rhode Island College, Certificate in Nonprofit Studies

Tennessee

University of Tennessee, Chattanooga, Certificate in Nonprofit Management

Texas

University of Dallas, Certificate for Not-for-Profit Management

University of North Texas, Graduate Academic

Certificate in Volunteer and Community Resource Management

Virginia

George Mason University, Certificate in Nonprofit Management, Certificate in Association Management

Virginia Commonwealth University, Graduate Certificate in Nonprofit Management

Virginia Tech, Nonprofit and Nongovernmental Organization Management Certificate

Washington

University of Washington, Nonprofit Management Certificate

West Virginia

West Virginia University, Nonprofit Management Certificate

Wisconsin

University of Wisconsin – Milwaukee, Graduate Certificate in Nonprofit Management

Continuing Education (CEU)

Arizona

Arizona State University, Nonprofit Management

California

California State University at Hayward, Non-Profit Management

California State University at Fresno, Nonprofit Leadership and Management

California State University, Fullerton, Leadership for Public and Nonprofit Service

San Jose State University, Nonprofit Management

University of California at Irvine, Fundraising

University of San Francisco, Executive Nonprofit Management, Development Director

Florida

University of South Florida, Nonprofit Management

Appendix

Indiana
> Indiana University – Bloomington, Nonprofit Management
> Indiana University, Center on Philanthropy, Fundraising Management

Maryland
> Goucher College, Nonprofit Management

Michigan
> Michigan State University, Excellence in Nonprofit Leadership & Management
> Oakland University, Nonprofit Management

Minnesota
> University of St. Thomas - Center for Nonprofit Management, Mini-MBA for Nonprofit Organizations

Missouri
> University of Missouri at Kansas City, Fund Raising Management

Nebraska
> University of Nebraska at Omaha, Fundraising Management

New York
> New York University - School of Continuing & Professional Studies, Fundraising
> The Union Institute, Certified Volunteer Manager

Oregon
> Portland State University - Division of Public Administration, Nonprofit Management, Nonprofit Development, Nonprofit Financial Management, Volunteer Management

Pennsylvania
> Bryn Mawr College, Executive Leadership
> Marywood University, Program in Non-Profit Management

Texas
> University of Texas at Austin - Thompson Conference Center, Management of Nonprofit Organizations

Virginia
> University of Richmond, Philanthropy

Washington
> Washington State University, Volunteer Management

West Virginia
> West Virginia University, Nonprofit Management

Wisconsin
> University of Wisconsin at Milwaukee, Professional Nonprofit Management
> University of Wisconsin at Superior, Nonprofit Administration

Online
> California State University, Long Beach, MPA
> Capella University, MS, Ph.D. in Human Services/ Management of Nonprofit
> George Mason University, MPA, Certificate in Nonprofit Management, Certificate in Association Management
> Indiana University-Purdue University-Indianapolis, Certificate in Nonprofit Management
> Regis University, Master of Nonprofit Management
> University of Colorado at Denver, MPA with Concentration in Nonprofit Organization Management
> University of Illinois at Chicago, Certificate for Nonprofit Management, School of Public and Environmental Affairs (SPEA), Nonprofit Management Certificate
> University of Maryland, Not-for-Profit Financial Management Graduate Certificate
> University of San Francisco, Development Director Certificate
> Walden University, MBA, MPA, Ph.D., Nonprofit Management and Leadership

INDEX

A

action verbs, 38-44
advisory council, 64
ageism issue, 58, 59
annual report, 29-30, 93, 96, 98
appearance, 26, 91
awards, 57, 59

B

Baby boomers, 28
benchmark setting, 13
Better Business Bureau's Wise
    Giving Alliance, 29
board member, 27, 62-66
board responsibilities, 63
body language, 92
business school, 69

C

career changer testimonials, 32-
33, 72-73, 106-107
career fairs, 25-26
certification, 59
chronological résumé, 51-52
combination résumé, 52
community involvement, 57, 58
computer skills, 59
conferences, 30
consultant
    assignments, 28-29
    entry to nonprofits, 68
    résumé builder, 27
corporate transitioners, 47, 67
corporate voluntarism, 69
cover letter
    dos/don'ts, 81
    e-mail, 81
    four-paragraph outline, 76-79
    importance of, 75-76
    language, 79-80
    samples, 82-87
Craigslist.org, 24

D

delegation skills, 49
diversity, 61

E

early retirees, 28
education
    assessment, 2, 4
    additional resources, 68-70
    business school, 69
    executive education, 69
    leadership program, 70
    résumé section, 35, 52, 57-58
    undergraduate/graduate
degrees, 69
elevator speech, 15-17
e-mail, 21, 23, 79, 81
employment online job boards,
21-23
Encore.org (Next Chapter), 28
executive
    education, 68
    search firms, 24-25
Experience Corps, 28

F

financial statements, 29
Form 990, 29, 90, 98
forums, 23-24
friend investment, 63
functional expertise checklist, 5
functional résumé, 52

G

give.org, 30
grade point average (GPA), 57-58
graduate degrees, 69

H

headhunters, 24-25, 36, 75
human resources, 64, 76, 90, 95

I

IndependentSector.org, 66
influence skill, 49
informational interview, 15, 17-
20
interest assessment, 8-9
Internet use, 21, 23, 59, 66, 81
internships, 27-28

interview
    appearance, 91
    body language, 92
    candidate questions, 98-100
    follow-up call, 103
    illegal questions, 58, 60, 95
    interviewer questions, 94-96
    lingo, 96-98
    post-interview reflections, 101,
    103
    pre-interview checklist, 99
    sample thank-you letter, 102
    sensitivity in, 91-92
    thank-you, 101
IRS Form 990, 29, 90, 98

J

job boards, 21-23
job search
    career fairs, 25-26
    cover letter, 36, 75-87
    e-mail application, 81
    executive search firms, 24-25
    follow-up, 101-103
    forums, 23-24
    informational interview, 15,
    17-20
    interest assessment, 8-9
    Internet use, 21, 23, 59, 66, 81
    internships, 27-28
    interview, 91-103
    job boards, 21-23
    networking, 11-17
    references, 104-105
    resources, 21-27
    salary, 88-90
    temporary staffing agencies, 27
    volunteering, 27-28, 66-67

K

knowledge investment, 63

L

language of nonprofits, 45-46
language, body, 92
leadership programs, 70

leadership skills, 49
libraries, 30-31
licensure/certification, 59
lingo, 96-98
LinkedIn, 23
listservs, 24
loaned executive programs, 67

M
management
    certificates, 70
    degree, 68
    skills, 49
    specialization, 70
money. See salary

N
National Charity Seal of
Approval, 29
networking
    board service and, 65
    buddy, 12-13
    elevator speech, 15-17
    forums, 23-24
    importance of, 11-12
    notes, 14
    thank-you notes, 17
    tips, 12-16
news resources, 30
Next Chapter (Encore.org), 28
Nonprofit FAQs, 31
nonprofit organizations
    annual reports, 29-30
    conferences/seminars, 30
    financial statements, 29
    language, 45-46
    leadership programs, 70
    libraries, 30-31
    management programs, 70
    news resources, 30
    Nonprofit FAQs, 31
    website, 30
nonprofit résumé example, 54

O
online job boards, 21-23
online networking, 23-24
on-the-job training, 7

P
personality checklist, 6
pictures with résumé, 60
political correctness, 61
post-interview reflections, 101, 103
pre-interview checklist, 99
professional achievements, 56
professional affiliations, 58-59
professional experience, 56-57
publications/presentations, 58

R
references, 104-105
résumé
    action verbs, 38-44
    boasting, 38
    cover letter, 36, 75-87
    current job description, 37-38
    examples, 53-55
    format, 51-52
    functional expertise, 47
    honesty on, 46
    improvement activities, 62-70
    irrelevant sections, 59-61
    language, 45-46
    length, 36
    numerical data, 36-37
    relevant sections, 52-59
    skill set, 2-7, 46-51

S
salary
    expectations, 88
    information resources, 90
    negotiations, 88-90
second career, 28
seminars, 30
Senior Corps, 28

skills
    assessment, 2-7
    corporate transferable, 48-51
    building, 65
    communication, 50
    delegating, 49
    functional expertise checklist, 5
    leadership, 49
    management, 50
    marketing, 65
    professional experience, 2-3
    transfer examples, 48

T
temporary positions, 27-28
temporary staffing agencies, 27
testimonials, 32-33, 72-73, 106-107
thank-you notes, 17, 101-102, 105
training, 24, 25, 28, 69

U
undergraduate degrees, 69
unemployment issues, 57

V
Voluntarism
    corporate, 69
    information through, 27-28
    loaned executive programs, 67
    resources, 68
    strategic, 67
    study on, 66

W
website, 30
work environment, 6

Y
Young Nonprofit Professionals
Network (YNPN), 23